Confoundin

Confounding the Mighty

Stories of Church, Social Class and Solidarity

Edited by
Luke Larner

scm press

© Luke Larner and Contributors 2023

Published in 2023 by SCM Press
Editorial office
3rd Floor, Invicta House,
108–114 Golden Lane,
London EC1Y 0TG, UK

www.scmpress.co.uk

SCM Press is an imprint of Hymns Ancient & Modern Ltd
(a registered charity)

Hymns Ancient & Modern® is a registered trademark of
Hymns Ancient & Modern Ltd
13A Hellesdon Park Road, Norwich,
Norfolk NR6 5DR, UK

British Library Cataloguing in Publication data
A catalogue record for this book is available
from the British Library

ISBN 978-0-334-06357-5

Typeset by Regent Typesetting
Printed and bound in Great Britain by
CPI Group (UK) Ltd

Contents

Section 3 'Casting down the mighty from their thrones': Class, Solidarity and the Struggle for the Common Good

Contributor Biographies

Ruth Harley

Ruth is a priest in the Church of England, currently serving her curacy in Milton Keynes. Before ordination she worked in the charity sector, and in parish-based youth and children's ministry. Ruth grew up in a working-class context in a small coastal town and was the first in her family to go to university. She is the co-author of *Being Interrupted: Reimagining the Church's Mission from the Outside, In* (SCM Press, 2020).

Luke Larner

A former bricklayer, Father Luke is a priest in the Church of England who has ministered in diverse parishes in Luton and Bedford with high levels of deprivation. A priest influenced by the radical Anglo-Catholic tradition, Luke's faith and ministry are shaped by a weaving of sacraments and social justice. He is currently studying for a doctorate in Practical Theology at the University of Roehampton. A tertiary Franciscan, Luke loves to be out in nature, cycling, kayaking or walking with his family, smiling at the birds and the trees.

Katherine Long

Katherine Long is from a rural working-class family. Her father was a professional driver and her mother was a cleaner and catering assistant. She was brought up in rented housing, initially private and then later a council house. Katherine has worked in a variety of fields, including as a cathedral verger, but settled into librarianship, both in public and academic libraries. Having felt a call to become a priest, in 2019 she was accepted for training for ordained ministry in the Church of England. She trained at Ripon College Cuddesdon and is now a curate in the north-east of England.

Sally Mann

Sally is the Senior Minister at Bonny Downs Baptist Church in East Ham (www.bonnydownschurch.org). She is the fourth of six generations of her family to live in the same East End neighbourhood. She has a PhD in Theology and is a Senior Lecturer in Sociology at Greenwich University. She is a co-director of Red Letter Christians, working to amplify the voices of grassroots leaders and activists working for Jesus and justice (www.redletterchristians.org.uk).

Eve Parker

Eve Parker navigates her working-class northernness in academia (often feeling like an imposter), currently as a Research Associate at the University of Kent, researching abuse in religious contexts. She is also Lecturer in Modern Christian Theology at the University of Manchester. Her recent publications include *Trust in Theological Education: Deconstructing 'Trustworthiness' for a Pedagogy of Liberation* (London: SCM Press, 2022) and *Theologising with the Sacred 'Prostitutes' of South India: Towards an Indecent Dalit Theology* (Leiden: Brill, 2021).

Rajiv Sidhu

Father Rajiv is a Church of England priest born and raised in a working-class world, getting his first manual job when his national insurance number arrived when he was 15 (though he'd been busy before that!). Growing up in a family of trades-people, market-stallers and shopkeepers, he knew the realities of intersectionality before he knew the word. As a British, Asian, cradle Anglican, the triangle of caste, colour and Christianity has never been far away. During his career as a teacher, and as Assistant Principal, he saw the myth that meritocracy offers, and its role in perpetuating structural injustices. As he entered ordination, caste, colour and Christianity intersected in new ways that were in direct opposition to the good news of the gospel, and the Magnificat. His priestly ministry is a quiet embodiment of liberative British Black Theology, of which his theological studies are part.

Selina Stone

Dr Selina Stone is Postdoctoral Research Associate in Theological Education at Durham University, where her research focuses on diversity and belonging. Her PhD in Pentecostalism and Social Justice is from the University of Birmingham (2021), and she has previously worked as a lecturer in theology and a community organizer. Dr Stone's working-class roots can be traced to her grandparents, who arrived in Birmingham from rural Jamaica in the 1960s and worked in the local foundries and as domestic staff. She was raised in Handsworth, inner-city Birmingham, and is a first-generation university student.

Victoria Turner

Victoria is a PhD Candidate in World Christianity at New College, University of Edinburgh. Her thesis looks at changing paradigms of mission in the contexts of class and coloniality. She is the editor of *Young, Woke and Christian: Words from a Missing Generation* (SCM Press, 2022), and further works in ecumenical circles and practical/public theology. Victoria grew up on a council estate in Cardiff, and prior to postgraduate study spent most of her time doing kickboxing and taekwondo.

Foreword

ANTHONY G. REDDIE

I am the eldest child of Noel and Lucille Reddie, Caribbean migrants who were part of the Windrush Generation. I was born in Bradford, West Yorkshire. My early formative years were spent in the predominantly White working-class area of East Bowling, BD4, one of the poorest wards in the city. My father was an ardent trade unionist and I was named after the famed Labour Party socialist MP, Anthony Wedgwood Benn, or Tony Benn in ordinary parlance. Noel was a member of the General and Municipal Workers' Union and at one point was a Works Convener. My mother was a part-time worker in a factory, then a housewife, later a cleaner and finally a dinner lady before she retired. My family lived in an unspectacular community of predominantly White working-class families. The six of us lived in a relatively small, terraced house, with an outdoor privy (toilet). Our neighbours were mainly part of the White working-class 'underclass', many of whom were unchurched and unemployed for several generations. I remember there being two dominant White families in the street, both with households consisting of three generations of people, all of whom were unemployed even during periods of full employment, when there was a surfeit of manual and skilled work in factories across the city.

My parents were hardworking and ambitious migrants whose modus operandi in moving to the UK was to make a better life for themselves and their anticipated children. During the cycle of a normal week there were two moments that differentiated our family from that of our White neighbours. First, in the early hours of a weekday morning, my father would leave our home at 5 a.m. to walk the four miles to work in a large industrial engineering firm. Most of his male peers would be in their beds sleeping off the excess of drunken nights in the nearby pub. The other moment of radical disparity was on a Sunday morning. Whereas many of our neighbours would sleep in, once again, shaking off the impact of too much alcohol the night before, the Reddie family would be up, resplendent in our Sunday best, heading off to church, in this case, Eastbrook Hall Central Methodist mission.

I offer these disparities between our family and our White peers, not to claim some kind of spurious superiority between us and them. Rather, it is to show some of the critical disparities that account for the changes in the lives of my family as opposed to those of our neighbours. It also explains some of the historic divergences between Black working-class and some White working-class peoples, and the resulting lack of solidarity between the two that has been deeply problematic on both sides.

When I reflect upon my upbringing in East Bowling the key reminiscence is one single moment from the long, hot summer of 1976. During the six-week holidays I asked my mother if I could 'play out' with some of the local White children. My mother was not keen and encouraged me to play with my siblings but not with the local White boys. My mother, an ardent and devout Christian infused with 'respectability politics' and ambition from imperial mission Christianity,[1] asserted that we were not like our neighbours. She then went on to explain that we were living in this, one of the poorest areas of the city, due to timing; Black working-class migrants coming to the UK often occupied the lowest rung in the socio-economic ladder in their first years in the country. It was her belief that the hard work, dedication and ambition thrust into us via our Christian formation in British Methodism[2] (allied to the Protestant work ethic) would enable us to leave the restrictive and bounded confines of East Bowling behind. Whereas our White neighbours had all lived in East Bowling for several generations, my mother was clear that we would be out in one generation.

At the time of writing, three of the four Reddie children are ensconced in middle-class professions, live in middle-class areas and have left East Bowling long behind. My mother's prophecy was correct. I have shared this narrative vignette in order to highlight the significant potency of this excellent book. The concept of 'race', while it is illusory, leads to the fact of racism as a socio-political phenomenon which is very real and has been long noted by Black and Womanist theologians. The manifest visibility of 'race', often associated with Black and darker skin, creates an unmediated sense of identification of those who are othered.

I write as an Oxford University academic theologian. I make my living as an educator, writing and speaking. I do not work in a factory with my hands as my father did. But I am still vulnerable to being othered as a social-political problem because of my Black skin. When I encounter the police, for example, apart from my facility to use big words, it is not immediately apparent that I am not the same Black working-class person I was in my youth. I am a Black man living in a postcolonial state that is riddled with systemic racism. But the fact is, I am not the same person as my youthful self growing up in East Bowling. My social class has changed.

It is the permeability of class that has made it a difficult and slippery phenomenon to explore theologically. Nothing in my formal theological education assisted me in making sense of my upbringing in East Bowling, Bradford. The people with whom I grew up were never going to write books or articles. Most of them never read books let alone write them. In order to write as working-class people, most of us have first had to become in some way middle class before we could find the space and resultant confidence to write our truth. That was certainly the case for me and perhaps for many of the participants in this excellent book.

The strength of this text is the way in which the various contributors all wrestle with the slippery nature of social class. If 'race' has been the solidified proverbial elephant in the room, social class has been the slippery eel. We have all recognized it but very few grasp and keep hold of it, notwithstanding the many who have spent much of their adult lives running headlong in the opposite direction. This fine text seeks to engage with this slippery eel in a respectful, generous and expansive manner. None of the writers are working on the assumption that their former selves were to be despised or looked down upon. All of them are aware of the losses in class terms in their own social and geographical journeys. Yes, class is often permeable, slippery and, given its often temporal nature for many who have been formed and socialized by means of education and academic study, an insoluble conundrum in terms of identity politics of solidarity (like many, in gaining an education I can no longer go back to East Bowling and belong as I once did), but this is no reason for it not to be taken with the utmost seriousness.

This is not a romanticized book. Father Luke Larner and his colleagues have fashioned a collection that is honest, compelling and not to be ignored. The wider church and theological education will do well to note the sharp learning to be accrued from engaging with this foundational text.

Anthony G. Reddie
Director of the Oxford Centre for Religion and Culture
Regent's Park College, University of Oxford

Notes

1 In using this term, I am speaking of a historical phenomenon in which there existed (and continues to this day) an interpenetrating relationship between European expansionism, notions of White superiority and the material artefact of the apparatus of Empire. This form of Christianity became the conduit for the expansion of Eurocentric models of Christianity in which ethnocentric notions of whiteness gave rise to notions of superiority, manifest destiny and entitlement. For a helpful dissection of this model of Christianity, particularly the British version of it, see T. J. Gorringe, 2004, *Furthering Humanity: A Theology of Culture*, Basingstoke: Ashgate. See also John M. Hull, 2014, *Towards the Prophetic Church: A Study of Christian Mission*, London: SCM Press.

2 I have written on the significance of this Christian formation on my subsequent social and geographical mobility in a previous piece of work. See Anthony G. Reddie, 2008, *Working Against The Grain*, London: Equinox, pp. 1–8.

Prelude

FR LUKE LARNER, EDITOR

I start this collection of stories, essays and conversations with a little bit of my own story. In academia we often call this 'reflexivity' – we locate ourselves in relation to our writing and research, sometimes by way of giving an apology for how awfully privileged 'we' are to be writing on a sensitive topic (social class in this instance). I share this bit of my story not as an apology, but simply to give some idea of the experiences I am writing from, because where you stand affects what you see. Some readers might resonate with this story, others might challenge my identification as working class, still others will read with interest while having had totally different experiences of class. All of the above are welcomed.

'You are what you're born'

Any time the topic of class was raised at home when I was growing up, my dad would respond with these words: 'You are what you're born.' It was like a family motto, meaning that no matter what happened in our lives, we were *always* going to be working class. This was nothing to be ashamed of, in fact quite the opposite. We were raised to be very proud of our family's humble roots. We were also raised to have a healthy suspicion of 'them' – the powerful 'other half' who did not live like us or share our values. I don't really remember much specific talk about the middle and upper classes, I just remember hearing a lot about this elusive 'them'. 'They' are not to be trusted, 'they' have never done a hard day's work in their life, 'they' have more money than sense and, as my nan Peggy Herne always used to say, 'You can't stop *them* shitting on you, but never let *them* rub it in.' This fear and disdain for the powerful became second nature to me, and many of my life experiences so far have taught me that it wasn't entirely misplaced. The suspicion of 'them' gave rise to a general distrust and dislike for school teachers, police officers, politicians and other symbols of authority. It made my dad's conspiracy theories about the sudden death of my uncle (a high-ranking trade unionist) seem plausible. It resulted in me inheriting a cheeky, rebellious attitude that has landed me in hot water on more than a few occasions, not least since working for the established Church.

Looking back over my life as I approach 40, I realize that my experiences of social class have, in reality, been far from straightforward. Both my parents left school young, neither went to university (my mum later did distance learning with the Open University in her 40s), and both had a humble start to life. But by the time I was born we were reasonably comfortable. My dad had worked his way up from being a printer's apprentice to the director of sales in a print company. He was a natural salesman, possessed of a mixture of working-class charm and good old Irish blarney from his mother's side. By the time I was four we lived in a respectable PVC-clad Wimpy house. It wasn't fancy, but it was ours (well, mainly the bank's). But as the saying goes, 'Easy come, easy go'. My parent's marriage ended and not long afterwards my dad was made redundant from his job. We couldn't pay the rent and he and I were left on the verge of homelessness. Those experiences shaped me a lot: the precariousness, the way we were treated when we looked for help, the disruption to my already turbulent education when we moved across town into a noisy council maisonette. Rags to riches, and back to rags again is all too easy when you don't have the safety net of family wealth.

In my late teens my life was in a downward spiral, and there was a danger that some of the things I was dabbling in could have gotten the better of me. In the midst of this, at the age of 16 I had a conversion experience in a little Baptist church with

Pentecostal leanings. There is no zeal like the zeal of a new convert (especially from a troubled background), and I jumped into Christianity with both feet, going to all the conferences, buying all the books and CDs, and becoming very committed to my local church. The freedom of adulthood loomed, and I remember declaring that the day I finished school was going to be the happiest day of my life. I was damned if I was going off to university to get into debt, suffering even more of '*them*' trying to brainwash me. My newfound faith added an extra dimension to my suspicion of '*them*', but also drove a wedge between me and my family.

Soon after finishing school, I disappeared off overseas with an international mission organization, making very little contact with home. After about a year of this I tried out being an informal 'intern' youth worker in a Pentecostal church. In my youthful fundamentalist enthusiasm, I didn't realize that 'intern' is code for labour exploitation, and that without money behind you, God's 'miraculous' provision (often in the form of envelopes of cash from wealthy and sympathetic members of the church) soon dries up. That old working-class suspicion of authority got the better of me too, and after a 'robust' theological dispute with the pastor, I left under a cloud. I couldn't understand why it hadn't worked out, I couldn't understand why I wasn't taken seriously as a leader. I remember one 'prophet' quizzing me about my family and educational background because he thought I had some sort of special calling. At no point in all of this did I even consider that the reason I wasn't taken seriously and didn't fit in with the other young Christian leadership hopefuls was because of my social class.

I became disillusioned, and after giving up on the idea of a life of 'ministry', I worked a few odd jobs to pay the rent on my room in a shared house. At one point I worked as a cook in a greasy-spoon cafe owned by a pastor. I remember the boss's wife noticing I had lost a lot of weight and asking me what my secret was. The answer I gave her was simple: 'I can't afford to eat.' If we wanted to eat while working, we were given just a measly 10% discount on the food ('Thou shalt not muzzle the ox' sprang to mind!). Not long after this I sort of drifted into becoming a labourer on a building site. I had just started dating my now-wife Jeni, who came from a trades family. A building site is a hotbed of class resentment, where skilled and so-called 'unskilled' people work hard in dangerous and unforgiving conditions for a fraction of the pay many of their customers make sitting behind a desk doing what Sally Mann describes in Chapter 7 of this book as 'bullshit jobs'. Both my body and my mind bear the impact and scars of many days working through pain, injury and exhaustion for fear of not making ends meet. You don't work, you don't get paid. This was the true precariat experience of living hand-to-mouth.

Many years later, I met the first Christian minister that I ever thought really took me seriously – a biker and minister by the name of Sean Stillman who ran Zac's Place, a 'church for ragamuffins' based in Swansea. 'God's Squad', the back-patch motorcycle club where I met Sean, became an important part of my life. It was the first time I was ever part of a Christian organization where I felt like I fitted in. The people 'got' me, and I them – it was intoxicating, almost dangerously so. When my wife Jeni and I heard Sean tell stories about their church for ragamuffins, we were hooked. Sean encouraged me to explore studying theology, and he and a couple of others helped reignite my earlier sense of vocation and my inquisitive mind for theology.

With Sean's help I applied to study part-time for a diploma in theology while still laying bricks four days a week. It was tough being so mentally and physically exhausted at the same time. I remember the anxiety when my first essay mark came back, and I quickly emailed my tutor to ask if a mark in the low 70s was a pass. That was when I realized I might have a knack for this theology thing, which was a surprise after how much I hated school.

To say that being given access to theological education changed my life would be a huge understatement – it turned my whole life upside-down. Before long I had given up my little construction business after about 10 years on the tools, and with the support of local churches and generous donors I was working full time as a lay minister in the centre of Luton, a rough-and-ready working-class town. We were living well below the poverty line on the grants and gifts people gave, but we survived. Becoming more closely involved in the Church of England made me realize just how big a problem class was going to be. I did not fit in at all, I found the culture baffling and at times offensive, and I certainly rubbed a few people up the wrong way (and still frequently do – sorry!). So when my pal Father Eddie took me out for a Nando's one day and popped the question – asking if I thought I might be called to be a priest – I laughed at him.

But here I am about five years later, a priest with a solid Master's degree, studying for a doctorate and now compiling a book. My life quite simply doesn't make sense to me anymore, and certainly not to the rest of my family. I was recently interviewed on BBC Radio 4 about class and church, and got a text from my Dad saying, 'Just listened, you sound more middle class than ever!' Radio 4 was not a thing in our house.

Two things changed when I got an education and became a minister. First, I realized the world wasn't as simple as I thought it was, and theology isn't as black and white as I thought it was. My mind was opened, maybe a little too much according to some. Second, through building friendships with people very different from me, many of whom were experiencing extreme marginalization, I realized that maybe I had a little more power and privilege than I thought. Like a classic 'white-van man', I used to half-jokingly ask, 'Where's all this white male privilege I'm supposed to have?!' Supported by patient and gracious friends who helped me learn, I soon realized that it was way more complicated than that. I learned that overlapping experiences of marginalization due to race, gender, sexuality, disability, and a whole raft of other intersections of identity alongside class, can add up to some major challenges. I realized, drawing from liberation theologies and the minds of people like Cornel West, Anthony Reddie and Monica Coleman, that instead of complaining, I needed to learn how to build solidarity and join others in organizing for justice. Those two pursuits have become a central passion and focus in life, ministry and my theological outlook. This passion has led me to involvement with causes such as homelessness and housing justice, the criminal exploitation of young people, support for sex workers, fighting for refugee and asylum-seeker rights, the trade union movement, broad-based community organizing and, more importantly, walking alongside a whole lot of people and supporting them in their own personal struggles for justice and dignity. Sometimes I've got it very wrong, sometimes I've been guilty of 'white saviourism', and I've still got a whole lot to learn. But I am certain of one thing: I have found the Divine in the midst of shared struggle, for 'God hath chosen the weak things of the world to *confound the things which are mighty*' (1 Corinthians 1.27 KJV). I would go as far as to say that the struggle for solidarity and justice *is at the heart of the mission of God*, but more on that later.

In the introduction to this book (Chapter 1), I will heavily critique what I call 'feckless faith'. A feckless theology of class is one that fails to recognize this drive towards solidarity and justice. I came to realize that without building shared solidarities in relationships with people different from me, I was doomed to this feckless faith. That is why I'm so grateful to have found such an amazing team of people to join with in creating this book. People with some vastly different experiences from mine, and some that are painfully familiar.

I hope you enjoy it, and that you will learn something of what I've learned from my co-conspirators in pulling this together. Special thanks go to David Shervington at SCM Press for first suggesting the book, and taking a risk on me as a first-time author.

This book is dedicated to my son Jared. I hope you have an easier time of it than I did, and make fewer mistakes than I have. Storm clouds are gathering in the world again, but I know that you have a heart filled with solidarity and a deep rage against injustice. Don't ever lose that, son; the world needs it.

SECTION I

'The Almighty has done great things for me': Intersectional Experiences of Class and the Church

Feckless Faith: Why the Relationship between Class and Christian Faith is a Justice Issue

FR LUKE LARNER

The Working Class is Back ...
and we refuse to be poor anymore.
(Mick Lynch, chairperson of the RMT Union)

It's fashionable to talk about race or gender; the uncool subject is class.
(bell hooks)

Introit

This book brings together the thoughts and experiences of a diverse group of theologians, activists and ministers, all of whom would in some way identify as working class. We have all had vastly different experiences of class, often related to other bits of the stuff that makes us *us*. This way of looking at class alongside other parts of our identity (such as our gender, ethnicity, sexuality etc.) is often called *intersectional* thinking. The term was coined by the American lawyer and scholar Kimberlé Crenshaw.[1] Crenshaw recognized that the way race, gender and class intersected in the lives of women like her resulted in particular challenges and compounded injustice. Class, as I will explore further, does not therefore exist in a vacuum – it cannot be studied under a microscope, separated from the way it interacts with a wider eco-system. Class is something that matters to a wide variety of people with distinctive life experiences and backgrounds.

As I will go on to explore, there is not a wealth of literature exploring faith and class in this intersectional way, particularly in British contexts. Even worse, there is a particularly lamentable lack of theological work exploring class intersections with an emphasis on solidarity and justice in British contexts.

This first chapter aims to set a scene for the chapters that follow. It is not by any means an exhaustive picture of church and class in twenty-first-century Britain, but rather it attempts to introduce how our present moment relates to a long history of class struggle. I will explore the relationship between religion, social class and intersectional solidarity, critiquing what I'm calling 'feckless faith'. I truly believe that investigating the topic of class is essential for our present moment. Mick Lynch, the firebrand leader of the Rail and Maritime Union, stated in a now infamous 2022 speech that, 'The working class is back ... and we refuse to be poor anymore.' The current strength of reaction, both positive and negative, to leaders like Lynch and the wider trade union movement demonstrates how key an issue this is for our time.

Classifying class?

Before going any further, it's important that I at least attempt a definition of social class. Class is a notoriously difficult concept to pin down. British culture has tended to divide people into three classes: working class, middle class and upper class. More recent research has suggested seven or more social classes in Britain, further complicating things.[2] Typically, class has been conceived of either in terms of how much power and/ or wealth someone has, or as a mere sociological and cultural phenomenon. These somewhat basic approaches have been rightly critiqued by those who wish to highlight the relationship between class and labour.

The German philosopher Karl Marx was hugely influential in defining social class in terms of labour relations. Someone is working class essentially because the surplus profit from their labour is being exploited by someone from a higher social class. In the most simplistic of terms, Marx defined class and the class struggle as being about labour relationships and the means of producing wealth. Working people have no access to the means of production and therefore can only make a living through selling their labour to those who own them. Those owners of the means of production then accrue their wealth and capital through the surplus generated from the labour of the workers. This is, of course, a gross over-simplification but this book is not an economic textbook. For more detail on this I highly recommend the first chapter of Joerg Rieger's edited volume *Religion, Theology, and Class: Fresh Engagements after Long Silence*.[3] I do not attempt to give a new definition of class in this introductory chapter; however, I do draw quite heavily on Rieger, and by extension Marx, in wanting to highlight the labour, economic and justice aspects of class (alongside cultural factors), and how they relate to church and theology.

As I will go on to argue, many other theological and church-orientated texts have tended not to make these emphases. Alongside this, I want to focus particularly on how an intersectional perspective demonstrates that class *cannot* be considered without paying close attention to other intersections of identity, particularly race. In addressing the relationship between race*ism* and class*ism* as unjust practices continuing to impact the lives of many people in Britain, I will begin to point towards our nation's political and colonial history.

The reason I wish to look at class in this broader perspective, possibly at the expense of a more narrowly defined and concise definition of class, is that I perceive a shallowness and failure to address the things that really matter in so much talk about faith and class. As I will go on to argue, a faith that does not engage with class in this broader sense fails to have much impact on the pressing issues of our time. A faith with a shallow view of class is, in my view, a *feckless* faith.

Why feckless faith?

The etymological root of 'feckless' comes from late-sixteenth-century variants of 'effect'. To be feckless means to be without effect, to be useless and lost. 'Feckless' is an insult, said with a smirk of mockery.

'Drunk, criminal, aimless, feckless and hopeless'

Reading these words, do any well-known Englishmen come to mind? In the year of our Lord 2022, one might think of the turbulent career of former Prime Minister Boris Johnson, and that would be half right. These words were not written *about* Boris, but *by* Boris. In 1995, he wrote that British working-class men are 'drunk, criminal, aimless, feckless and hopeless' and have 'low self-esteem brought on by unemployment'.[4] Ironic given Boris's own recent employment history.

Twenty-five years after writing this, Boris commissioned a report as prime minister investigating why 'white working-class boys' were falling behind their peers in school and being 'let down'. These are emotive terms – 'let down' implies a degree of care and a perceived injustice. So why did Boris switch from being a cynical mocker of working-class males to speaking out to support them and their education? Was this a change of heart? Sadly, I think there was a more sinister agenda. The report claimed that use of the term 'white privilege' has 'contributed towards a systemic neglect of White people facing hardship'.[5] Those who keep a close eye on such things will notice the classic tactic by which powerful people blame the plight of one marginalized group on another marginalized group, stoking hatred and shifting the responsibility away from those with decision-making power. Describing 'white privilege' as a 'politically controversial terminology', the report suggests schools using it fall short of their duties under the Equality Act 2010.[6] This report reads like a thinly veiled threat attempting to inhibit how schools address racism. One Conservative MP even suggested that teachers caught using the term should be reported to the Home Office for extremism.[7] So what started out looking like a bit of class solidarity turned out to be a trojan horse in the so-called 'war on woke' and part of the slow dismantling of critical thinking in British education. This is one of many examples of the populist 'culture war' politics that have come to polarize societies in so much of the Western world.

Boris's sham solidarity towards 'white working-class boys' can help us understand wider trends in class discourse by exemplifying a lack of intersectional perspective. In her book *Where We Stand*, the late, great bell hooks suggested that, while it is 'fashionable to talk about race or gender; the uncool subject is class'.[8] In the next section of this chapter, I will reflect on *Where We Stand* using intersectional conversations about class in twenty-first-century Britain. An often-overlooked intersection of identity in these conversations is religion. In 2013, Joerg Rieger described a 'long silence' in discussions of religion and class.[9] Drawing from my own experiences as a former bricklayer and now Church of England priest and theologian, I will explore 'disturbing the sound of silence' (which is what we intend to do in this book). It's important to say, however, that inspired by liberation theologies my co-authors and I wish not merely to *reflect* on our situation, but to *transform* it.[10] With this in mind the final section of this chapter acknowledges that we gather as theologians, ministers, organizers and activists *'not to mourn, but to organize'*.[11]

We write this little book in solidarity with workers, scholars and world-changers of all faiths and none, while rooted in our own perspectives and experiences. For me, this means writing from my own perspective as a white, working-class male Christian (there are, of course other 'bits' of me that make me *me*). I will go on to address how faith relates to those described as 'feckless' by the powerful by drawing from the Christian concept of *kenōsis* – a 'self-emptying' or 'non-grasping'. This relationship between *kenōsis* and feckless faith will help us explore where we stand, disturb the sound of silence and move from mourning to organizing. My co-authors will develop these themes further in their own chapters, which are arranged in three main sections:

Section 1: 'The Almighty has done great things for me' – in this section we explore our own intersectional experiences of class, faith and church.

Section 2: 'Lifting up the lowly' – this section explores class and leadership in the mission and ministry of British Christian communities, identifying struggles and barriers to the participation of working-class people in leadership.

Section 3: 'Casting down the mighty from their thrones' – in this section, we highlight that desire 'not to mourn but to organize' by exploring how to struggle for solidarity, justice and the common good as Christians, churches and other organizations.

Where We Stand

As I have already begun to describe, in twenty-first-century Britain, class discourse is closely interrelated with racism and other intersections of oppression. Class does not exist in a vacuum and therefore cannot be addressed alone, especially from a theological perspective. When I read phrases like 'traditional working-class communities' in some texts, I'm reminded of the British Black Liberation theologian Anthony Reddie's question, 'When did working-class become code for white?'[12] Ruling elites have long fostered and exploited the relationship between racism and classism. In his 1935 book exploring the history of American reconstruction from 1860 to 1880, W. E. B. Du Bois looked at the relationship between black working-class and white working-class workers and exclaimed, 'There probably are not today in the world two groups of workers with practically identical interests who hate and fear each other so deeply and persistently and who are kept so far apart that neither sees anything of common interest.'[13] In 1964 Bob Dylan sang that 'The poor white man's used in the hands of them all like a tool', and is 'only a pawn in their game'. The British rapper and social commentator Akala traces the history of elites 'legally privileging all people racialised as white' to 'buy the racial loyalty of poor whites'.[14] What these very different voices agree on is that racism is directly related to classism and labour exploitation, as Selina Stone will demonstrate at length in Chapter 5. A painful local example of this came when a trainee vicar applied for a post not far away from me, and was turned down. The reason given was that, coming from a majority-world heritage, he might not feel comfortable ministering in a so-called 'white working-class area'. While it was recognized as a 'poor choice of words' in a public apology, this incident underlines that issues of race and class are closely related.

Class and whiteness in post-Brexit Britain

The relationship between class and whiteness has become especially fraught in post-Brexit Britain. The government's feigned concern for 'white working-class boys' is a classic example of the wealthy and powerful blaming the poverty and powerlessness of the so-called 'white working-class' on working-class people from majority-world heritages. As Anthony Reddie rightly argues, it's 'ridiculous and insulting' to think 'that rich conservative politicians are in solidarity with the poor'. The poverty experienced by poor white people is not the fault of 'other poor people from the Global South or from Eastern Europe', but rather is the result of a 'skewed system'.[15] To my shame it took me many years to realize that by exploiting this relationship between class and whiteness, powerful people consolidate their power by getting oppressed groups fighting over the crumbs from the master's table.

The artist Grayson Perry, whose work on class and masculinity I have found helpful, describes the way working-class bodies are perceived as 'chaotic and grotesque' in comparison to the tightly buttoned-up middle-class body.[16] There is a long association between being working class and being somehow chaotic, dangerous and even criminal. Despite his later efforts at gaining white working-class votes, Boris Johnson's description of British blue-collar men as 'criminal' is highly ironic coming from the first-ever British prime minister to have been found to have broken the law while in office. I expect this trend of political criminality to continue as certain sections of our society wrestle more and more with a post-imperial melancholia that laments the perceived loss of the so-called 'glory days' of empire when Britain dominated much of the globe.[17] In such contexts of nihilistic despair, Cornel West charts the way people often turn to 'unprincipled abuse of power' in order to 'gain or retain power'. As Britain's so-called glory days fade into distant memory, there are those at the top who will go to almost any lengths to shore up their power rather than let it dissipate. Gaining and retaining power in this way is a gangster-like behaviour, and when this behaviour is perpetrated among elites like Johnson and his cabal, it is an elite gangsterism.[18] This anti-democratic gangsterism can be found in many areas of society, including in the established Church.

I recently watched the 2019 Guy Ritchie film *The Gentlemen*, which is a fascinating portrayal of social class and gangsterism in the UK through a typically violent tale for the genre. I found it particularly interesting in that it not only explores the relationships between class, criminality, education and culture, but it also seems to fall into some familiar traps in the portrayal of British working-class culture, including that the main (anti-)heroes of the story are 'hard' white men. The film tells a lurid tale of dodgy deals, 'gentlemen gangsters' (of whom I've known a few myself), working-class crooks trying to be accepted by the upper classes, and people hustling for money and power through criminality and violence. Reflecting on class and gangsterism as I watched this film led me to one conclusion: be it elite or street, gangsterism's hustle for money and power is ultimately the sad triumph of self-interest over solidarity.

Class is a relationship

Wealthy Conservative politicians support an economic system that perpetuates existing socio-economic divides. By exploiting the fears of working-class people and stoking racial tensions, they are effectively trying to run a protection racket to stay in power. This is exemplified in the 'invasion' rhetoric we have heard from successive Home Secretaries with regard to immigration. Despite what these racketeers would have us believe, working-class people do not need them or their exploitation. As Rieger demonstrates, class is a *relational* term: there is only a working class because there is are a middle and an upper class who are getting wealthy off the backs of workers.[19] When working-class people of all intersections recognize that these class relationships are oppressive and unjust, they will demand their overthrowing. When those of us who are inspired by the Christian liberation tradition make this recognition, we will see that *God* also desires those class relationships to be overthrown.

In my own preaching and organizing, I have at times experienced myself and others being described as 'adversarial' and even 'aggressive' in our passion for justice. But despite how passionately I believe in God's 'preferential option for the poor', I believe that class justice is actually good news for everyone in the long term (although it might not feel like good news to the oppressors initially, as it will cost them!). In seeking the overthrow of these unjust class relations, we might sing with Blessed Mary that God 'has cast down the mighty from their thrones and lifted up the lowly'. This casting down and lifting up is ripe with the promise of post-liberation reconciliation. Maybe the casting down of some and the lifting up of others allows for the possibility of meeting in the middle.

Disturbing the sound of silence

'Divide and conquer' has always been the playbook of elite gangsters, both imperial colonialists and neo-liberal gangster capitalists. Here Christianity's part in all this becomes clearer. There are deep-set beliefs behind Britain's sense of self-importance. There is a dangerous 'Rule Britannia' ideology behind popular anthems such as 'Jerusalem':

> Bring me my bow of burning gold!
> Bring me my arrows of desire!
> Bring me my spear: O clouds unfold!
> Bring me my chariots of fire!

I will not cease from mental fight;
Nor shall my sword sleep in my hand
Till we have built Jerusalem
In England's green and pleasant land.

The militaristic words match a stirring swell of pride driven
by the musical composition. This is manifest destiny: Britain is
seen as God's own country and brave souls are ready to fight
for it.[20] As Reddie suggests, Brexit and the rise of nationalism
inherit this very logic of British exceptionalism from 'imperial
mission Christianity' and its self-proclaimed mission from God
to conquer the world with Christianity, Commerce and Culture.[21] But recent trends in British politics have convinced me
that the so-called 'white-man's burden' to conquer the world
and remake it in our own image never went away. When elite
gangsters in the present day wish to consolidate their political
and economic power through a colonial drive with its roots
in the mission history of western Christianity, working-class
Christians should be wary, especially those of us having our
whiteness appealed to.

This is, of course, not a uniquely British problem. Christian
nationalism and Christo-fascism are on the rise around the
globe. The title of this chapter, 'Feckless Faith', is in part a
parody of *Reckless Faith*, a book (ironically) about discernment.
Its author, the US evangelical John MacArthur, proclaimed 'any
true Christian will vote for Trump' – the archetypal neo-liberal
gangster who showed off about his sexual exploits. Despite
this, White evangelicals in America overwhelmingly supported
Donald Trump; many saw him as 'God's anointed' and some
still do. This may look like a uniquely American problem, but it
seems to me that the relationship between White evangelicalism
and right-wing neo-liberal gangster politics in the USA is also
influencing the UK. American evangelical leaders have a huge
influence and following here through speaking tours and the use
of media, and this influence is present in the established Church
too. An example that seems almost stranger than fiction was
when the now-disgraced mega-church superstar Brian Houston
was invited to give the keynote speech at one of the most influ-

ential leadership conferences in the Church of England in 2020, soon after hustling his way into a photo op with Trump in the White House and recording a glowing video endorsement for him. I expect we will see more and more obvious examples of this problematic relationship between right-wing politics and religion unfold over time.

Letting go – class and *kenōsis*

I have talked about disturbing the sound of silence with regard to church and class, and in this vein I will now offer an alternative discourse to this, rooted in the Christian concept of *kenōsis*.

In Christian theology, *kenōsis* comes from the description of Christ's incarnation in Philippians chapter 2: Christ 'did not regard equality with God as something to be grasped, but emptied himself, taking the form of a slave, assuming human likeness' (Phil. 2.6–7 NRSV). The words 'emptied himself' (*kenōo*) are often extrapolated into a general ethic of 'self-emptying', which Christians are called to practise. Here I want to distinguish between *kenōsis* as self-emptying and the Anglican theologian Sarah Coakley's conception of *kenōsis* as 'non-grasping of certain types of worldly power'.[22] The former might seem to suggest that Christian *kenōsis* calls the exploited working classes to empty themselves of what little they have, allowing the powerful to continue their exploitation. After all, was not Christ himself a willing victim of an oppressive empire? As Coakley and others recognize in the context of *kenōsis*, and Rieger in the context of class, there is a flow of power here that needs interrogating.[23]

In *The Making of the English Working Class*, E. P. Thompson argues that there is a long relationship between Christianity and the flow of class power in England. In his view, a key moment came when the French Revolution raged on the continent but the energies of working-class uprising in England were dissipated in the Methodist revival. He suggests that while the revival created opportunities for working-class people to become organized and self-educated, the emotional and spiritual energies of impending revolution were 'confiscated for the service of the Church' in 'orgiastic revival meetings' leaving workers less resistant to the drudgery of industrial labour.[24] The erotic and phallic imagery here resonates with the critiques that Linn Marie Tonstad has made of conceptions of *kenōsis* as a form of self-emptying. While Thompson's argument seems a little one-sided, given the early roots of the labour and union movements in Methodism and non-conformism, still today theologians like Robert Beckford have observed that Christian faith can leave people too heavenly minded to be any earthly good.[25]

Coakley also describes *kenōsis* as space-making: opening oneself up to be delighted by the 'other'. These heteronormative erotic undertones exemplify another way that bad theology can impact the working classes. Thompson critiqued Methodism as a movement *for* the working class, not *of* the working class, which is largely still true of many Christian movements that claim solidarity with the working classes today.[26] The danger of rooting a theology of class in a *kenōsis* that emphasizes this heteronormative concept of space-making is that it can become overly focused on church reproduction.[27]

Two popular but narrow issues

This obsession with reproduction is shown in much contemporary Christian literature addressing class and church, often with a focus on two specific 'issues'. The first issue is congregational growth. The key question becomes, 'Why aren't there many working-class people in church?' Here I'm reminded of Reddie's question about class and whiteness because these discussions tend to overlook the congregational make-up of black majority Pentecostal churches, which are often significantly working class (as Selina Stone points out in her chapter). There appears to be a conflation of 'working class' and 'white' in what is being looked for. Despite popular reception, the recent book *Invisible Divides* by Natalie Williams and Paul Brown seems to fall foul of this with its focus on a 'general overview of class in Britain today' that intentionally excludes a focus on how class intersects with race, gender and other areas.[28] In doing this the book tries to paint working-class culture in hugely broad strokes, when in reality there is a vast amount of diversity in working-class cultures, especially when other intersections are considered.

There is a disturbing trend among some books looking at church and class. *Unreached* by Tim Chester focuses on 'growing churches in working-class areas' and *Invisible Divides* focuses on class 'barriers to belonging in the church' for people 'saved from working-class backgrounds'.[29] To paraphrase Reddie, I wonder what part of being working class people need saving from? I would suggest that the reproductive drive to build, plant and grow churches in so-called working-class areas or 'estates', without any emphasis that God is calling us to shift class relationships towards justice, is another form of labour exploitation. It seeks to use the money, time and labour of working-class people to enable the church-planting agendas of others, often middle-class senior church officials. On top of this, the colonial mindset of imperial mission Christianity is present once again: there is almost no acknowledgement of the fact that a significant proportion of working-class people in Britain find their spiritual home in faiths other than Christianity.

The second issue mirrors the dynamics I identified in English politics as pitting class against other intersections of identity to further an agenda. The key question here might be, 'Why doesn't the Church care as much about white-working-class suffering?' The Anglican Gary Jenkins suggests that the Church has focused on 'race ... gender and sexuality, rather than class' and that 'working class people themselves have been overlooked ... because of a deep rooted prejudice against working class people ... endemic in British culture'.[30] While Jenkins recognizes that not all working-class people are white, this rhetoric suggests a zero-sum game in which class issues are in competition with 'race and gender', despite the inextricable links between the three being clearly demonstrated in intersectional theory. This zero-sum approach to class and other intersections of oppression is, of course, not unique to theological discourse. In his otherwise excellent book *Poverty Safari*, the Scottish rapper and social commentator Darren McGarvey argues that class remains the primary dividing line in our society, and suggests that 'as intersectionality has become more prominent, class analysis has been discarded', seemingly conflating intersectional discourse with a shallow identity politics.[31] As I have already argued, I believe it is impossible to address class without considering other intersections, and this does not mean abandoning critical class analysis. I agree with the Indian Marxist K. Murali that 'proletarian interests' should not be separated as 'something sectional', but that as Marxism has always taught, 'the prole-tariat can achieve its liberation only through the emancipation of all humanity', which means addressing the 'emancipatory concerns of all oppressed and exploited sections of society'.[32] Our class struggles ought to be in solidarity with all of our oppressed siblings as we work and hope for liberation.

I've noticed that a common tactic in church discourse on this second issue is to reference so-called 'working-class atti-tudes' to Brexit. Both Jenkins and the Anglican bishop Philip North point to a major divide between working-class people who are strongly in favour of Brexit and the anti-Brexit 'liberal middle-class elites' who supposedly run the Church.[33] A pop-ular study suggests that around 64% of working-class people voted for Brexit, compared with around 49% of 'middle-class', hardly a massive contrast. The latest surveys suggest that only 23% of working-class people think Brexit has benefitted the UK, and only 42% now think we were right to leave, yet this divisive narrative is perpetuated.[34] As a working-class person myself, I find it insulting to be caricatured and spoken for in this way, especially by middle-class leaders.

So how do these issues and the inclusion and championing of the working class in church relate to *kenōsis*? Tonstad describes how a space-making logic of *kenōsis* undergirds a desire for church reproduction, either through 'new birth' or 'inclusion'. Tonstad challenges an 'inclusion' that presupposes an 'other' on the outside of the Church's 'inside circle', because Jesus Christ was crucified outside the city gate among those we would deign to 'include'.[35] As the Sri Lankan liberation theologian Aloysius Pieris recognizes, the Christ of the Poor is found among those we might try to include or convert, and in contexts like his and mine, a large proportion of Christ's poor seek their ultimate meaning outside the western Christian tradition.[36]

The Inclusion Paradox

Here I return to Rieger's relational conception of class. Rieger challenges class 'inclusion' among other intersections of identity, because class is 'not a matter of God-given diversity' but is 'produced in a conflictual relationship, whereby the power and success of one class is built on the back of the other'.[37] Celebrating diversity in terms of class, as Williams and Brown do, compounds the problem by 'endorsing differences' that 'benefit some more than others'.[38] Our task, therefore, is not to champion or include more working-class people in the Church, but rather take part in the prophetic critique and the overthrowing of unjust class relationships. Indeed, in recognition of God's preferential option for the poor we might realize that *Jesus Christ has chosen a side in the global class struggles.* My own Church has, I believe, failed to recognize this, a sin closely related to its collusion in imperial and colonial mission history.[39]

Without this recognition of the danger of inclusion when it comes to class, a kenotic theology of class becomes an opiate of the masses in its most negative sense by 'including' working classes in a Church that makes them too heavenly minded to be any earthly good. This is a feckless faith: a faith without effect, a faith that writes books on church and class without once mentioning the words 'liberation' or 'capitalism'. A feckless faith that calls people 'saved from working-class backgrounds' to 'empty themselves' and take up their place within a Church indifferent to its master's mission to cast the mighty down from their thrones and lift up the lowly (Luke 1.52).

So can Christian faith (especially through the emphasis on *kenōsis*) only further oppress the working classes through peddling feckless faith, or is there an alternative?

'Not to mourn, but to organize'

As a former bricklayer, practical theologian and busy parish priest, I have little use for armchair theology that 'can count every hair in the beast's coat, but never look it in the face'.[40] Drawing from the emerging interdisciplinary field of working-class studies, I desire to join others 'not to mourn, but to organize'.[41] Working-class studies uses auto-ethnography, emphasizes intersectional perspectives, and is a form of 'praxis and class struggle, not just an academic exercise'.[42] I believe, therefore, that there is exciting potential for dialogue between theology and working-class studies, which is rooted in building intersectional solidarity and organizing for change. That work exists beyond the pages of this chapter, where it will be refined by the other writers contributing to this book, and tested in the streets as we struggle together for our shared future. I will, however, make some closing observations, specifically relating back to the theme of *kenōsis*.

If feckless faith can be fuelled by a *kenōsis* of self-emptying and space-making, might a *kenōsis* of non-grasping offer an alternative? Coakley's conception of non-grasping relates to Christ's example of unwillingness to grasp certain forms of 'earthly' power.[43] While I find this idea useful, I believe it is enriched by Tonstad's alternative: 'co-presence'.[44] Co-presence emphasizes relationship. For me the key to non-grasping and co-presence is in the relationships of solidarity that working-class people of all intersections might build among themselves and with others who wish to take part in the journey from the world as it is to the world as it should be. Cornel West describes the vital importance of building solidarity across lines of difference, recognizing that it is not easy work.[45]

Of tremendous potential in this drive for solidarity are the many religious traditions that emphasize non-grasping and co-presence through spiritual practices that transform our relationships with others and the world. *Kenōsis* has, for example, been a bridge in my own dialogue with Zen Buddhist friends whose emphasis on detachment and the relational reality of the 'no-self' has impacted me tremendously. While this has been explored in Jewish, Buddhist and Christian dialogue, I hope to see further work, particularly with Muslim friends and colleagues who have been so important in the recent campaigns and activism that I've engaged with.[46] One such example came in the work of the Muslim Liberation theologian Sharaiz Choudry, who co-chaired the inaugural European Academy of Religion panel on class, where this chapter was first shared as a shorter paper.

Conclusion

There is no more time to squabble over the crumbs from the master's table; our existence and the future of our species depend on grass-roots practitioners, activists, scholars of religion, faith leaders, artists and many others learning the hard graft of building global solidarities that can navigate difference.[47] A Christian theology of class must be ready to accept this challenge while recognizing the historic injustices perpetrated by our tradition, which so often sought to dominate, convert or eliminate our others. The alternative is a feckless faith that fails to recognize that the relationship between church, theology and social class is not an issue of inclusion, it is an issue of justice and a matter for repentance.

In this chapter I have made some introductory comments about where we stand, I have attempted to set the stage for my co-authors to disturb the sound of silence and, most importantly, I have tried to emphasize that we as authors gather 'not to mourn, but to organize'. If we were to add up all the stories of class struggle, activism and organizing that my co-authors and I have experienced, this book would be far too long. But we offer it as part of an ongoing conversation that I hope to see amplified and diversified in the coming years, in the hope that Christian conversations about class are no longer characterized by feckless faith.

Notes

1 Kimberlé Crenshaw, 'Mapping the Margins: Intersectionality, Identity Politics, and Violence against Women of Color', *Stanford Law Review*, 43.6 (1991).

2 Michael Savage, 2015, *Social Class in the 21st Century*, London: Pelican, p. 177.

3 Joerg Rieger (ed.), 2013, *Religion, Theology, and Class: Fresh Engagements after Long Silence*, New York: Palgrave Macmillan.

4 Boris Johnson, 1995, *The Spectator*, 19 August, p. 6.

5 Education Select Committee, 2021, 'The Forgotten: How White Working-Class Pupils Have Been Let down, and How to Change It – Education Committee – House of Commons', p. 15.

6 Education Select Committee, p. 19.

7 Harry Taylor, 2021, 'Tory MP Says Using Term "White Privilege" Should Be Reported as Extremism', *The Guardian*, 9 October, https://www.theguardian.com/politics/2021/oct/09/tory-mp-says-using-term-white-privilege-should-be-reported-as-extremism (accessed 6.01.2023).

8 bell hooks, 2000, *Where We Stand: Class Matters*, New York and London: Routledge, p. vii.

9 Rieger, *Religion, Theology, and Class*.

10 Gustavo Gutiérrez, 1988, *A Theology of Liberation: History, Politics, and Salvation*, Maryknoll, NY: Orbis Books, p. 12.

11 Michele Fazio, Christie Launius and Tim Strangleman, 2021, *Routledge International Handbook of Working-Class Studies*, Routledge International Handbooks, Abingdon and New York: Routledge, p. 1; emphasis added.

12 From an unpublished paper at the 2021 'Dismantling Whiteness: Critical White Theology' conference.

13 W. E. B. Du Bois, 1935, *Black Reconstruction*, New York: Harcourt, Brace & Company, p. 700.

14 Akala, 2019, *Natives: Race and Class in the Ruins of Empire*, London: Two Roads, p. 63.

15 Anthony Reddie, 2019, *Theologising Brexit: A Liberationist and Postcolonial Critique*, Routledge New Critical Thinking in Religion, Theology and Biblical Studies, London and New York: Routledge, p. 171.

16 Grayson Perry, 2017, *The Descent of Man*, London: Penguin Books, p. 67.

17 Paul Gilroy, 'Joined Up Politics and Post-Colonial Melancholia', *Journal of Contemporary African Art*, 2000.

18 Cornel West, 2005, *Democracy Matters: Winning the Fight Against Imperialism*, London: Penguin, p. 59.

19 Rieger, *Religion, Theology, and Class*, p. 10.

20 I am indebted to Sanjee Perera for her work on this.

21 Reddie, *Theologising Brexit*, p. 70.

22 Sarah Coakley, 2002, *Powers and Submissions: Spirituality, Philosophy and Gender*, Challenges in Contemporary Theology, Oxford and Malden, MA: Blackwell Publishers, p. 10.

23 Coakley, *Powers and Submissions*, p. 22; Rieger, *Religion, Theology, and Class*, pp. 13–14.

24 Edward P. Thompson, 1966, *The Making of the English Working Class*, New York: Vintage Books, pp. 368–9.

25 Robert Beckford, 2021, *My Theology: Duppy Conqueror*, London: Darton, Longman & Todd, pp. 77–8.

26 Thompson, *Making of the English Working Class*, p. 37.

27 Linn Marie Tonstad, 2017, *God and Difference: The Trinity, Sexuality, and the Transformation of Finitude,* Gender, Theology and Spirituality series, Abingdon and New York: Routledge, pp. 266–8.

28 Natalie Williams and Paul Brown, 2022, *Invisible Divides: Class, Culture and Barriers to Belonging in the Church*, London: SPCK, p. 15.

29 Timothy Chester, 2012, *Unreached: Growing Churches in Working-Class and Deprived Areas*, Nottingham: Inter-Varsity Press; Williams and Brown, *Invisible Divides*, front matter (in fairness to the authors this phrase comes from the publisher's synopsis not the content of the book itself).

30 Gary Jenkins, 'Where Are the Working Class?', *Psephizo*, 2020, https://www.psephizo.com/life-ministry/where-are-the-working-class/ (accessed 22.03.2023).

31 Darren McGarvey, 2018, *Poverty Safari: Understanding the Anger of Britain's Underclass*, London: Picador, pp. 122–3; 154.

32 K. Murali, 2020, 'The Vanguard in the 21st Century', in *Of Concepts and Methods*, Paris: Foreign Languages Press, p. 100.

33 In Madeleine Davies, 2021, 'Is the C of E Still a Class-Riddled Act?', *Church Times*, 25 June.

34 YouGov/The Times Survey Results, 24 May 2022, https://docs.cdn.yougov.com/m5m97b82y6/TheTimes_VI_220525_W.pdf (accessed 22.03.2023).

35 Tonstad, *God and Difference*, p. 276.

36 Aloysius Pieris, 1988, *An Asian Theology of Liberation*, Edinburgh: T & T Clark, p. 87.

37 Rieger, *Religion, Theology, and Class*, p. 11.

38 Williams and Brown, *Invisible Divides*, pp. 151–4; Rieger, *Religion, Theology, and Class*, p. 11.

39 Reddie, *Theologising Brexit*, p. 27.

40 Leonardo Boff and Clodovis Boff, 1987, *Introducing Liberation Theology*, Maryknoll, NY: Orbis Books, p. 17.

41 Fazio et al., *Handbook of Working Class Studies*, p. 1.

42 Fazio et al., *Handbook of Working Class Studies*, p. 14.

43 Coakley, *Powers and Submissions*, p. 11.

44 Tonstad, *God and Difference*, p. 106.

45 Cornel West, 1999, *The Cornel West Reader*, New York: Basic Civitas Books, p. 408.

46 See John B. Cobb, Christopher Ives and Masao Abe, 2005, *The Emptying God: A Buddhist-Jewish-Christian Conversation*, Eugene, OR: Wipf & Stock.

47 Catherine Keller, 2021, 'Spiritual Foundations of One World', *Contribution to GTI Forum Can Human Solidarity Globalize?*, https://greattransition.org/gti-forum/global-solidarity-keller (accessed 22.03.2023).

2

Wandering in the Wilderness: Education, Class and Dislocation

REVD RUTH HARLEY

It is the end of my first term at university. I am at a drinks party in my tutor's rooms. I am trying to pretend I like red wine, and wondering if the dress I'm wearing, which I bought in a charity shop yesterday, counts as a cocktail dress. I'm not really sure what a cocktail dress is, except that it's what one of my new friends told me I should wear to something like this. I've never been to something like this before. My tutor, an extremely eminent man in our field, walks over and joins the conversation that I am hovering on the fringes of. He laughs at my class-mate's joke that I don't understand. He exchanges pleasantries with another student about a few of their mutual acquaintances whom I have never heard of. Then he turns to me and says, 'I've been meaning to say, Ruth, I should lose that accent if I were you. Nobody will take you seriously sounding like that.'

This is neither the first, nor the last, nor the most profound moment of alienation I experienced as a working-class young woman in academia. But it is perhaps the one that has had the most impact on me. Because I did what he said. I tried to lose my accent. And I almost succeeded, although I still never sounded quite like the posh people around me. It's something I have regretted for most of my adult life.

It has also given me a metaphor for my experience of becoming a very well-educated working-class woman: it's like 'becoming bilingual – I speak fluent "middle-class" ... but it is not, and never will be, my mother tongue'.[1] Like many people who acquire fluency in another language, and move to inhabit another culture, I have lost a little bit of my fluency in my mother tongue. I speak 'working class' with a hint of a middle-class accent now. There is nowhere I am effortlessly culturally fluent.

I have often wished I could go back and tell my 18-year-old self to stand her ground, be herself, and not take this crap from anyone (however eminent). I wish I could tell her that the reason she doesn't fit in is not because there's anything wrong with her, it's because the forces of classism and sexism are stacked against her. But I don't think she'd be ready to hear.

Like many working-class young people whose brains happen to work in a way that aligns well with the demands of formal education, I had been offered – and had accepted – the idea that education could be my 'ticket out of here'. If I worked hard enough and did well enough, I could escape. What that escape would look like and where I would be escaping *to* was something I had only the haziest idea of. I just knew I wanted something more and something different from life than what seemed to be available where I grew up. At the height of the Blair years of 'education, education, education', and before student debt became anything like as burdensome as it is today, university seemed like a possible route – indeed, the only possible route – to that elusive 'something more'.

In this chapter I will begin by exploring the sense of dislocation that my experience as a working-class young woman encountering the alien world of higher education generated (and to some extent has continued to generate). I will reflect on that sense of dislocation in relation to the scriptural and theological landscape of the wilderness, and specifically in relation to the narrative of the Exodus. I will then explore some of the sociological and theological assumptions underpinning the narrative of 'social mobility' in relation to young people who are (as I was) working class and educationally high-achieving, and how some of those theological and sociological underpinnings are also expressed in the church's approach to and understanding of working-class communities. Finally, I will offer solidarity as an alternative to the 'social mobility' model.

This solidarity is underpinned by the vision of the Magnificat. I will reflect on how this vision might help address questions of class, education, and the intersection between them.

Dislocation – wandering in the wilderness

It would be years after my own dislocating experience of higher education before I could acknowledge that in looking to gain 'something more' I had also lost something. I watched (via Facebook) my peers bringing up their children in the same streets where we grew up, surrounded by the network of family, friends and neighbours that had provided such grounded stability to my own childhood. I realized I had lost that grounded stability for myself and any children I might one day have. I had lost that sense of rootedness, of unquestioned belonging, of mutual support and trust. It had gone, along with my accent, and there was no getting it back.

I do not want to romanticize the reality of working-class communities like the one I grew up in. I certainly do not want to suggest there is anything good or beneficial about the kind of poverty that grinds you down and keeps you so focused on where the next meal, the next rent payment, the next electric top-up is coming from. That stops you even beginning to look towards 'something more'. That level of poverty is crushing, soul-destroying, dehumanizing. And we must never lose sight of the fact that it is the result of political choices made by those who will never come anywhere near to experiencing its consequences.

But I do want to draw attention to the giftedness of working-class communities like the one I grew up in. Working-class communities are frequently framed primarily in terms of deficit, as 'needy' or 'deprived'. Too often this comes from middle-class people who have never got close enough to see them for what they really are. It is language that all too often pervades how the church speaks of these communities too. One of my tasks as a working-class priest-theologian is, I think, to point to the abundance to be found in working class communities, to be attentive to the ways in which God is present and active within those communities, and the ways they resemble the kin-dom[2] of God.

Understanding the giftedness and abundance of the community I left behind has been, for me, an essential component of articulating the profound sense of dislocation that I felt as a young woman entering the deeply alien culture of an 'elite' university. That sense of dislocation is something that I have continued to experience (though far less acutely) throughout my adult life. As my appreciation for God's presence, agency, abundance and blessing in the lives of working-class communities has expanded and deepened, I have been able to acknowledge the process of loss and grief that came with leaving.

That *grief* is part of the sense of the dislocation that has characterized my experience of being a working-class woman with access to an unusually high degree of education. Another component of that dislocation has been the sense that I am not 'supposed' to experience the move from straightforwardly working-class belonging to a far more complex non-belonging in terms of loss as well as gain. The narrative of social mobility is one of one-directional 'improvement'. And it goes, of course, hand-in-hand with the idea perennially levelled at working-class people, that we should 'be grateful' for any access we have to the world beyond our communities of origin.

Dislocation is an uncomfortable experience – that sense of belonging neither here nor there, of being neither one thing nor the other. But it is also an experience with plenty of precedent in Scripture and in the lives of the saints. In Scripture the experience of dislocation is very often expressed through the landscape of wilderness, and that wilderness is a theologically rich landscape in which to dwell.

The theological landscape of the wilderness

Wilderness is a recurring landscape in the narrative of Scripture. In the wilderness, Jesus is led by the Spirit, tempted by the Evil One and ministered to by angels. In the wilderness, John the

Baptist calls the people to repentance, to prepare the way of the Lord. In the wilderness, the Psalmist bears witness both to the faithful guidance of God,[3] and to the unruliness of God's people.[4] In the wilderness Elijah, like many prophets before and after him, experiences both despair and comfort.

The wilderness is a site of divine revelation, of God's nearness and guidance, of the leading of the Holy Spirit. It can be harsh and even desolate, but it is also transformative. Very often theologians and pastors have been quick to equate wilderness with 'spiritual dryness' or 'losing the way' – a site of lack or need, rather than gift or abundance. But the landscape of the wilderness, like the landscape of the council estate or the Urban Priority Area, is a landscape of abundance if only we will enter it with eyes and hearts open to its particular gifts.

In the tradition of Godly Play, stories that take place in the wilderness (and there are many of them) traditionally start with a reflection on the landscape itself:

> So many wonderful and important things happened in the desert, we need to know what it is like ... The desert is a dangerous place. It is always moving so it is hard to know where you are. There is little water ... People do not go into the desert unless they have to.[5]

This exemplifies the paradox of wilderness. It is risky, insecure and very often unchosen, and yet it is also the site of 'wonderful and important' encounters with God.

In the wilderness with Moses: wandering towards the promised land

Of all the scriptural stories of wilderness, the one that most resonates with my own experience of the wilderness of not-belonging in which I have found myself as a well-educated, working-class woman, is the story of the Exodus. Moses and the people of Israel leave the hardship of slavery in Egypt and wander in the wilderness for 40 years in search of the promised land. As they wander, they find that the wilderness is a land-scape rich with unexpected and surprising encounter with God.

There are times when they long to go back to where they were before, although they know the flaws and dangers of that situation.[6] There are times – many times – when they cannot imagine what it is they are going on to, or how they will get there. There are times when they create new kinds of space on the journey for encounter with God[7] and times when encounter with God in the wilderness takes them entirely by surprise.[8]

All of these sorts of experience I could map on to my own wandering in the wilderness where class and education inter-sect. I do not think I realized until it was far too late that it would not be possible to go back, or that there would ever be a time when I would long to do so. I have still not worked out, and perhaps never will, quite what or where it is that I am going on *to*. But this wilderness has been and continues to be a site of encounter with God. Often that encounter has been unexpected and startling, sometimes a source of comfort but at least as often a source of further dislocation – that sense of being driven or led into the wilderness by the Holy Spirit. And there has also been the need to find new ways of intentionally encountering God, new ways of relating to God and relating my experience of God to my experience of dislocation and discomfort.

Moses, of course, never quite gets to the promised land. He is continually journeying, continually heading towards that elu-sive 'something more'. And there is a resonance there with my experience too. Whatever I have left behind, in terms of step-ping beyond the bounds of a straightforwardly working-class identity and experience, I have not 'arrived' at some alternative. There is, of course, a limit to the analogy with the Exodus – and certainly I do not want to hold up 'becoming middle class' as in any way equivalent to the 'promised land'! (Although perhaps there are echoes of that in how the idea of education as a 'way out' was presented to me as a young person.) But there are also resonances to be explored: the leaving of a place in search of 'something more', only to discover that neither the journey nor the elusive 'destination' are quite what we expected. And yet God is in it.

Education and social mobility: an individualistic narrative

The story I internalized about education, as a working-class girl who did well at school, goes something like this: You are clever (surprisingly clever for someone with your background). The way we know you are clever is because you do better than your peers in tests and exams. And because you are clever, you have a chance to make something of your life. You can use that cleverness to get out of this place. Because you are clever, you have opportunities to do more and achieve more and have more than you ever could in the place you come from, the place you're 'getting out' of. You can do well if you work hard. If you work hard, you can do just as well as the kids from other, posher places (the ones whose cleverness is a birthright rather than a surprise). Education is your ticket out of here. It can change your life. It can change you.

All narratives contain assumptions. There are many assumptions in this narrative, some of them more obvious than others. There are many ways in which I might now critique this narrative. Below are some theological critiques that I (as a priest-theologian) offer to this narrative and the assumptions underpinning it:

Assumptions about cleverness. Clever, intelligent, bright, smart … these are words often applied early and uncritically to children, as are their rather less flattering opposites. They are value judgements, which make it clear to children (and adults) that some people are seen as more valuable than others. A mind that works in a particular way is set up for 'success' while a mind that works in a different way is set up for 'failure'. The person, in all their complexity, is reduced to a particular skill set or way of performing, which fails to take a holistic view of who they are and what they are capable of. People are valued primarily for (a very limited subset of) what they can do, rather than the fullness of who they are: beloved creatures made in the image of God.

Assumptions about achievement. Achievement in this narrative is assumed to be competitive, hierarchical and measurable. This is such a pervasive set of cultural assumptions that it is often almost invisible. Yet the God of the Christian faith works in the small and the ordinary, in the mustard seed and the bruised reed. The God I believe in works in and through what seems like failure to the world – even the ultimate failure of a painful and humiliating death. Faith in this God, then, surely calls us to resist and disrupt these assumptions about what achievement and success look like.

Assumptions about social mobility. Social mobility is, in this narrative, assumed to be both possible (for some) and unquestionably good. There is no space for nuance, no room to acknowledge the value of what is left behind, and certainly no room to question whether 'getting out' is really the right option. There is no space here for acknowledging the ambiguity and grief that accompany any significant life change. A belief in God who accompanies us through all the joys and challenges of life, and is big enough to encompass every experience and emotion, opens us up to a more nuanced and ambivalent reading.

Assumptions about community. Community is not mentioned at all in this narrative. Most charitably, we might say that it is ignored or seen as unimportant. Perhaps more accurately, it is seen as subservient to the interests of the individual. Working-class community features only (implicitly) as that from which the individual can, and should, 'get out'. There is an absolute absence here of any concept of community as either gift or necessity. Yet a trinitarian theological framework must surely see it as both. God who is love, who exists in perpetual relationship, calls and draws us into that loving relationship too. For Christians, community is not an optional extra.

Individualism and interdependence in the church

Individualism, competitive achievement, disregard for community – we might like to think that these are hallmarks of a flawed, 'worldly' narrative, but we are kidding ourselves if we think they are not present in the church. Indeed, they are especially present in a church that uncritically adopts many of the assumptions of the middle-class culture in which it is embedded. So how might some of the assumptions we have seen embedded in narratives around education, social mobility, class and community work themselves out in the life of the church?

Individualism is a common feature of some contemporary church cultures, including some that have a significant reach and influence in the UK context. An emphasis on a 'personal relationship' with Jesus, at the expense of acknowledging the centrality of interdependent community/communion in the life of the church, can tend to lead to a conflation of spiritual growth with personal development and/or fulfilment.

The assumptions of the narrative of personal relationship as the primary expression/experience of faith has something in common with the assumptions of the narrative of social mobility as the primary function of education. In both cases the agency of the individual is at the heart of the narrative, to the extent of sidelining and marginalizing the role of the community: of the church in the former case, and the working-class community in the latter. In both cases the narrative is significantly distorted and impoverished by failing to account for the centrality of community, both in the life of the church and the life of working-class young people.

In the case of the church, the centrality of community/communion is essential to the life of the Christian. The corporate nature of the church, as the body of Christ, is inseparable from what it is to be a disciple of Christ. Pauline ecclesiology, with its focus on the interconnected nature of the body of Christ, finds its clearest expression in 1 Corinthians 12:

> For just as the body is one and has many members, and all the members of the body, though many, are one body, so it is

with Christ. For in the one Spirit we were all baptized into one body – Jews or Greeks, slaves or free – and we were all made to drink of one Spirit. Indeed, the body does not consist of one member but of many.[9]

As Paul notes, no member of the body can say to another 'I have no need of you.'[10] Interdependence is inherent in the nature of the church, and where an emphasis on individualism undermines that, it is to be resisted. Paul's ecclesiology is by no means unproblematic. Feminist theologians have critiqued his imagery of Christ as the 'head of the body' for being hierarchical.[11] This is worth bearing in mind in the context of any sort of class analysis. But Paul's emphasis on mutuality and interdependence within a diverse body does act as a strong corrective to individualism.

Social mobility or solidarity?

As we have seen, the model of 'social mobility' that underpins the narrative into which I bought as an academically high-achieving working-class young woman is deeply theologically (as well as sociologically) flawed. It positions education as a means of escape, of betterment, of 'getting out' and finding 'something more'. It rests on an underlying dynamic of competitive achievement, and also of scarcity. If I could 'get out' it was on the assumption that most of my peers must be 'left behind'. The dynamic of scarcity operates here on two levels. First: the assumption that there is only so much 'social mobility' to go round, that it is inherently something from which only a minority of working-class young people can ever benefit. Second: the assumption of scarcity within our working-class communities of origin, that these communities are solely a site of need and lack, rather than gift, and are therefore something to be escaped from.

Both these assumptions of scarcity should be challenged by a theology that sees God, and God's creation, as a site of abundance. They rest on an unspoken assumption that people must be in competition with one another, that 'succeeding' at the expense of those 'left behind' is both possible and desirable. This assumption is at odds with a vision of creation and of human flourishing that sees mutual interdependence as inherent in God's will for God's creatures; a vision that finds its expression in – among other things – Pauline body ecclesiology.

The second assumption – that working-class communities are a site of need rather than gift – is perhaps even more theologically pernicious. To assume that there are some communities characterized solely or primarily by scarcity is to assume that there are limits on where and how the underlying giftedness of God's creation is expressed. To assume that scarcity (the kind of lack that makes somewhere a place to escape from) can be straightforwardly aligned with material poverty comes dangerously close to equating material wealth with abundance, gift and even blessing.

Those of us who live or have lived in working-class communities know that they are sites of God's grace and abundance, that they are full of often undervalued gifts – in terms of people, culture, stories, networks and so much more.[12] Yet within a predominantly middle-class church these communities continue to be viewed primarily through the lens of need and scarcity. They are instrumentalized as on the 'receiving end' of both material help and 'mission',[13] rather than viewed as the sites of God's abundant gift and grace that they are.

Part of my experience as a working-class priest whose educational privilege (and changed accent!) very often lead me to be read as middle class has been to have to explain over and over that my own sense of calling to ministry in working-class communities has nothing to do with having a benevolent 'heart for the poor'. It has everything to do with longing to participate in the abundant life of God that I encounter in those communities. It is a conversation I have had many times, with many senior clergy, and one I will no doubt continue to have, unless a significant theological shift from assumptions of scarcity to assumptions of abundance can be made within the church.

So what is the alternative to the sort of scarcity-based model that leads to the promotion of 'social mobility' as a/the 'solution' for working-class young people whose minds work in a way that aligns with the demands of higher education? What kind of vision does an abundance-based theology generate for working-class young people longing, as I was, for 'something more' than what they see around them? The key concept here is, I think, solidarity. Solidarity, the understanding that our lives and struggles are bound up in one another's, is a key sociological concept for class politics, but it is also an expression of the sort of inextricable mutuality and interdependence that finds its theological expression in Pauline ecclesiology of the body of Christ.

Solidarity is, in many senses, the opposite of social mobility. Where social mobility rests on an assumption of scarcity and competition, solidarity rests on an assumption of collaboration. And though a framework of abundance is not essential to the concept of solidarity, it is certainly compatible with it in a way that it is not with social mobility. If we believe in a God of abundance rather than scarcity, a God whose gifts are to be found and expressed in our interconnectedness and interdependence with one another and the whole creation,[14] then it is to solidarity rather than social mobility that we must turn.

A church in the shape of the Magnificat is necessarily one that turns towards solidarity, towards collaboration and shared struggle, and away from individualistic 'success'. But what, then, of that working-class young person yearning for 'something more', as I was? The Magnificat is in many ways the exemplary expression of that yearning. But in it, the 'something more' is something collective, the overturning of unjust power for the liberation of the whole creation, rather than something individualistic.

The yearning for 'something more' in a world that seems to offer working-class young people so little is an expression of divine discontent, akin to that expressed by Augustine: 'You have made us for yourself, and our hearts are restless until they find their rest in you.'[15] It is a restlessness that can drive us out into the wilderness, seeking 'something more'. The individualistic 'something more' of achievement, success, betterment, escape can only ever really be a panacea. We are still in the wilderness, still seeking and yearning after 'something more', something we cannot find in our own strength or abilities but only in turning and returning to God, who draws us into community, into radical solidarity, to seek that 'something more' not in self-sufficiency but in mutuality and interdependence.

The capitalist, class-ridden society in which we live would have us direct our yearnings for 'something more' towards individualistic self-improvement and social mobility, to 'getting out' and getting on in ways that ignore or reject the importance of community. And in doing so, it would draw our attention away from the power of solidarity to both speak and enact a yearning that is not for individual 'betterment' but for collective transformation towards a more just and more liberated/liberating social order.

A church which is complicit in that individualistic narrative is one that will channel our yearnings for 'something more' solely or primarily towards developing a personal relationship with God and finding/creating a worship experience that fulfils and uplifts us as individuals. And in doing so, it will distract us from the collective vision of a Magnificat-shaped kin-dom of justice and peace in which our mutual interdependence is valued as the gift and blessing it is.

When I think of my 18-year-old self, standing awkwardly in an ill-fitting cocktail dress and wondering how I could ever fit into a world that had no space for my voice, this is the vision I would like to offer her: *To set my own sense of dislocation and not-belonging, my own longing for 'something more', in the context of God's longing for justice and transformation.* Working-class young people are sold short when we are sold an individualistic vision of education as a means of 'getting out', which leaves us wandering in the wilderness. We and our communities deserve something more expansive, more abundant, more reflective of the wideness and wildness of God's grace, more honouring of the gift of who we are in all our complexity, our creaturely frailty and our divine giftedness. And we deserve a church that can see us for the God-given gift we are, rather than trying to form us into something we are not.

Notes

1 Al Barrett and Ruth Harley, 2020, *Being Interrupted: Reimagining the Church's Mission from the Outside, In*, London: SCM Press, p. 22.

2 Following the convention of many feminist theologians and others committed to moving away from hierarchical assumptions, I choose to use 'kin-dom', with its connotations of mutuality and interconnectedness, rather than 'kingdom', with its connotations of patriarchal rule and control.

3 For example, Psalm 78.52.

4 For example, Psalm 106.14.

5 Jerome W. Berryman, 2002, *Godly Play: Volume 2*, New York: Morehouse Education Resources, Church Publishing Inc., p. 60.

6 Exodus 16.3.

7 Exodus 40.

8 Exodus 19.17–25.

9 1 Corinthians 12.12–14.

10 1 Corinthians 12.21.

11 Natalie K. Watson, 2008, *Introducing Feminist Ecclesiology*, Eugene, OR: Wipf & Stock, p. 43: 'It [the metaphor of church as both body and bride of Christ] shows the utter dependence of the feminine church on its male head, Christ, a disembodied man.'

12 Cormac Russell, referenced in Barrett and Harley, *Being Interrupted*, pp. 133–4.

13 For critiques of the power dynamics involved in 'mission', see John V. Taylor, 1992, *The Christlike God*, SCM Press, pp. 260–4, further explored in Barrett and Harley, *Being Interrupted*, pp. 68–72.

14 Amy Plantinga Pauw, 2017, *Church in Ordinary Time: A Wisdom Ecclesiology*, Grand Rapids, MI: William B. Eerdmans Publishing, p. 45.

15 Saint Augustine, trans. Henry Chadwick, 1998, *Confessions*, Oxford: Oxford University Press, p. 3.

3

Caste, Class and Colour:
The Church's Triangle of Tragedy

FR RAJIV SIDHU

In this chapter I explore the intersectional relationship between caste, class and colour within a Church of England context. All migrant populations face the challenge of navigating their cultural heritage alongside assimilating to the culture within their new home. Within a South Asian context, this primarily focuses on the engagement with caste and British culture. Yet there are further challenges, navigating belief and faith within this south Asian culture. Socio-economic standing is another barrier to overcome, the diversity of migrants reflecting the full range of social classes, confounding the stereotypical caricatures of all migrants being poor refugees, or even politically liberal. There are the culture clashes, both home and abroad, as caste and class set the stage for conflict. Race and racism provide the third angle in this triangle of tragedy that migrant populations face as they are judged by the colour of their skin before anything else. Here I examine each of these issues. Each, on its own, is a difficult challenge for the church to relate to. When the three issues of caste, colour and class combine, in a multifaceted intersectional experience, the reality within this triangle is tragic in the true sense of the word; because the world and context in which this occurs does not offer the resources to help navigate the realities of this experience. Or simply put, what are the odds that your local Church of England parish is able to help with someone navigating this reality? Caste, class, and colour truly confound the mighty.

Immigrants and their baggage

Broken by the empire, raised by MTV
Misfit of the motherland, still fish and chips for tea
Broken by the empire, raised by MTV
But still, it's fish and chips for tea.
(Lady Parts, 'Fish and Chips')

This raucous chorus resonates with the passion and rage of the diaspora experience. The Channel 4 comedy *We Are Lady Parts* captured the joys and sorrows of navigating the diaspora existence within modern Britain, following each character's confrontation with culture and encounter with exclusion. The whole melting pot of the diaspora experience is sampled within this one lyric. How do British Asians navigate their past and integrate it with their future?

While the show focused on the Muslim experience of four girls in the punk band Lady Parts, the challenges are common to the British diaspora experience. Caste, class and colour join in a dance of exclusion that transcends cultural boundaries. A multifaceted identity does not protect from further exclusion, rather it invites it. Can one be 'British' with brown skin? Not without battling racism – structural, implicit and ignorant. But for those who return 'home', their caste and colour again define their place in the world. And what of the working-class East London accent, which betrays your upbringing? A childhood of shopping in Shoe Zone is not a common experience within academia, or indeed within the clergy of the Church of England.

I am writing from a particular vantage point. I am a British Indian assistant curate within the Church of England. I am a cis-gendered male, which gives me certain privileges when I am in the room. Yet at the same time, my own working-class background and ethnic heritage leads me to encounter situations that I experience as racist, classist and casteist. These experiences all take place within Christian settings, which seems to perpetuate the opposite of a belief in the *imago Dei* and the *missio Dei*.

Post-George Floyd, the church has done much to signpost its affirmation of cultural diversity. The *Lament to Action* report is to be lauded for bringing to the fore over 30 years' worth of recommendations to challenge racial injustice within the Church of England.[1] Yet at the same time, there is always more work to be done, to acknowledge that each person is human, beautifully made in the image of God. Much has been discussed about racial justice within the Church of England, although much of this focuses upon what could be crudely described as colour-lines: 'Black Versus White'. James Cone and Anthony Reddie argue convincingly that to be ontologically black is to be the other, to be those who are oppressed and marginalized.[2] There is a place for this, and it is an important space within the discussion surrounding justice. Gustavo Gutiérrez argues the same – the poor are those who have to 'fight for life'.[3] Those who are at the margins are included in the broad label.

But what of the differences within the labels? And what of the discussion surrounding this within the Church of England? In his exploration of Dalits (the lowest, 'untouchable' caste in the Indian caste system) and Christianity, Sathianathan Clarke notes that Dalit conversations surrounding justice tend to exclude the Adivasis (a collective name for indigenous tribal groups who are some of the most oppressed in India).[4] Writing in her book *Azadi*, Arundhati Roy pronounces a devastating critique of India's whitewashing of Gandhi, and its ignorance of Bhimrao Ramji Ambedkar (who led the drafting of the independent constitution of India), who, unlike Gandhi, was very critical of the caste system. To be silent in the time of oppression is to side with the oppressor. But to be able to engage with this discussion, we first have to make a brief foray into the caste system within India, or Brahmanism as it is rightly called.

Roy explains Brahmanism as: 'a brutal system of social hierarchy ... Institutionalised cruelty which has survived more or less intact from ancient times.'[5] She elaborates:

what the anti-caste tradition calls Brahmanvaad – Brahminism. Brahminism organizes society in a vertical hierarchy based on a supposedly celestially ordained, graded scale of purity and pollution, entitlements and duties, and hereditary occupations. Right on top of the ladder are Brahmins, the embodiment of purity, the resting place of all entitlement. At the bottom are the 'outcastes' – Dalits, once known as Untouchables, who have been dehumanized, ghettoized, and violated in unimaginable ways for centuries. None of these categories is homogeneous, each is divided into its own elaborate universe of hierarchies. ... Even today, caste is the engine and the organizing principle that runs almost every aspect of modern Indian society.[6]

Roy's acknowledgement of the elaborate universe of hierarchies is key. Within Brahmanism there is infinite room for social exclusion and marginalization. And this extends to those of other nations; with Brahmanism purveying the belief of one God, one nation, one soil. The interplay between Brahmanism and fascism in India and Indian politics is both obvious, and dangerous to comment upon. What does this mean for the UK?

Simply put, the lenses and the means of engaging with ethnic and cultural difference within the Church of England do not allow for a conversation surrounding racism within global majority communities. Roy highlights Gandhi's racism towards black Africans in 1894, and the hypocrisy of Brahmanism claiming a common stock – 'the Indo Aryan' – while at the same time arguing for the freedom of the 'Hindu homeland' from the occupation of Muslims and Christians; that is, foreigners. This cultural baggage is exported, and imported into all diaspora communities, alongside chillies, spices and saris. Indian Christians comment upon the skin colour of other Indian Christians, creating a market for the skin-bleaching creams that are readily available in all South Asian stores, who import them from the subcontinent. Blatant racism exists within the Indian diaspora community, against and towards others; usually targeted towards black Caribbean communities. Guz Khan's use of his platform to challenge this on the *Big Narstie Show* (which has a global majority viewing audience) highlights the conversations within the communities around exclusion, Brahmanism and casteism. But within the Church of England this conversation does not exist. Instead, culture and identity are brushed into broader criteria that are unable to engage with differences. As Lady Parts later scream:

I'm a P.O.C.
B.A.M.E.
D.O.A.
P.T.S.D.

Roy is clear – class and caste are similar, but not the same. And it's true. The girls in Lady Parts are not only misfits of empire but they are also misfits in their home culture, reduced to three- and four-letter acronyms. Depending on their social standing within the class system of the UK, they too may face further persecution and trouble. In *Empire's Endgame*, eight British scholars document the reality of racism and the British state that stokes racism and anti-immigrant rhetoric.[7] As Cornel West affirmed in an interview on the David Letterman show, 'black faces in high places' doesn't change much. This is a sentiment echoed in Reddie's assessment of the (then) newly elected British Cabinet, invoking Zorah Heale Hurston's phrase 'all my skinfolk ain't kinfolk'.[8] Diaspora populations have a wide diversity within them; caste being one example of this within the South Asian community. An intersectional perspective demonstrates that caste alone is not the only barrier that diaspora migrant communities face within the United Kingdom context.

A question of class

The Church of England's engagement with the working classes is also challenged and problematic. Grass-roots voices, such as the Twitter account Estate Ministry, demonstrate the gulf between church words and church action with regards to addressing the inequalities existing in modern Britain today. It is said that theological colleges used to have elocution lessons to ensure that clergy sounded appropriate, and things haven't changed all that much. The church continually struggles to reconcile liberation theology and other streams of Christian social teaching with its place of power and privilege within the state and the nation.

David Edwards, in his *A Concise History of English Christianity: From Roman Britain to the Present Day*, outlines the historical legacy of Victorian social culture in moulding the Church of England today; with the poor being unable to access the habit of regular churchgoing, explaining that 'To many manual workers and their families such a habit was unthinkable: they did not possess the necessary beliefs or morals, education or energy, clothes or cash to rent pews (as was often necessary).'[9] Being a Christian is an expensive habit. Edward Norman, in his exploration of 'the Victorian Christian Socialists', describes how Brooke Fosse Westcott was encouraged by the growth of religious sympathies in all the classes against the presence of evil, considering 'the suitability of the church for service as the agent of social regeneration'.[10] Throughout her history, the Church of England has wrestled with the exclusion that arises from power, privilege and wealth. The ground-breaking 1985 report *Faith in the City* sought to address social issues facing the modern church and revealed some of this tension. Sadly, it assessed and then dismissed the potential contribution that liberation theology could make to the Church of England, arguing that it had little to offer in a 'developed' context like England.[11] In direct contrast, Father Joe Williamson, Father Dolling and Father Kenneth Leech are all historical examples of socially conscious clergymen (predating the ordination of women). I am inspired by women like Reverend Sophie Cowan, Mother Kath Black and Bishop Lynne Cullens, who continue that legacy today.

But these inspirational leaders remain outliers. In many ways the established church's engagement with those on the poverty line today can be described, in the words of rapper Plan B, as an 'urban safari'. Plan B's lyrics describe the feeling of being on the outside, never being inside, never being fully engaged. He describes as hopeless the experiences of young working-class people who 'ain't never getting out' of the deprived areas where they are raised. Young people whose aspirations are limited by those who should encourage them to dream bigger. For me these words encapsulate the experience of being a working-class person within the Church of England.

So far, we have met two aspects of the church's triangle of tragedy. On the one hand, we have the challenge and reality of being ill-equipped to engage with the spectre of Brahmanism and cultural imperialism within the global majority congregation of the Church of England. On the other hand, we have briefly explored the exclusion and isolation that class creates within the Church of England.

Colour – a Black and White issue

Last but not least is the experience of being in a different race within the Church of England. I firmly believe that this is the driving force behind the differences in experience within the church. The contrast between Jarel Robinson-Brown and Calvin Robinson's approaches to racism (the former affirming the existence of institutional racism; the latter denying it) is due to the cultural imperialism that is entangled with class and race.[12] You might wonder if someone with a rich, white-sounding name is ever going to experience the same pushback as someone with a poor, foreign-sounding name.

Assistant curates occupy a particularly vulnerable role as 'apprentice ministers' in the Church of England. Recent events have already demonstrated that race is a factor in assistant curate posts not being offered to people, or posts being withdrawn, and posts failing. A now infamous BBC *Panorama* documentary investigated the role of racism within the Church of England, leading to multiple failed curacies; in each of these, race was directly identified as a driving force for failure. Much work has been done following the release of this investigation; yet as the *Lament to Action* report highlighted, there have also been at least 30 years' worth of unfollowed recommendations and delayed hope.

Even the recent positive movements within the Church of England's General Synod, shining a spotlight on work towards racial justice, came with a sombre warning from the Diocese of London's racial-justice priority group member, Prebendary Amatu Christian-Iwuagwu, who pointed out how empty the chamber was during the discussion.[13] Justice is difficult to find when no one else joins you at the table to discuss it.

The purpose of this chapter is not to discuss the full extent of the tragedy of racism in the Church of England, nor is it to discuss the full extent of the tragedy of class issues within the Church of England. There are other, better-informed and more deeply engaging texts that explore this. But the point of this chapter is to shine a light on the intersectionality of oppression and marginalization when race, class and caste intersect within the Church of England, creating a triangle of tragedy. When the institution has no words, understanding or means of engaging with the different aspects of this. When all that is left is the rage of Lady Parts' chorus and the anger of Plan B's verse. Reaching again into a discography of discontent, Riz Ahmed offers an insight into this triangle of tragedy. He raps about the tension between his upbringing in a Britain where people drink tea and neo-nazi skinheads continue the appropriation of the swastika, both of which come from the place where his 'DNA is at' but which he has never called home.

The threads of injustice, colonialism, persecution and indifference weave themselves into the tapestry that forms diversity in many of our dioceses. But there is no excuse for not engaging, not exploring and not acting in situations of oppression. Kimberlé Crenshaw's understanding of intersectionality demonstrates, clearly within the legal sense, the role that multiple identities have in amplifying exclusion.[14]

What then should the church do? What is the action to take? Will changing the content of the Durham Common Awards modules (which many candidates training for ordination study) help resolve this issue? Will placements in other cultures resolve this issue (as new guidelines suggest)? Could engaging in postcolonial thought, as championed by Sugirtharajah, help resolve these issues? Well, not if Sethi and her critique of the politics of Postcolonialism are to be believed; whereby 'Postcolonialism' has become a byword replacing 'Third World', and where black and brown faces within academia continue to be 'lonely onlys'. 'Postcolonial' has become a byword for 'foreign' and 'exotic'. Some people, such as Kwok Pui-lan, find the lens of Postcolonialism helpful in identifying, critiquing and dismantling the influence of empire within theology and the Church of England.[15] But in a political landscape where far-right politics and priorities continue to flourish and grow in Britain and Europe, the political theology of Dorothy Sölle and her understanding of 'Christofascism' are more persuasive to me.[16] A theology that engages xenophobic hate with individual agency. These are all issues that continue to confound the mighty, and lead to the marginalization of the most vulnerable within our churches.

So what should the church do? Well, a hopeful practical ecclesiology for a secular age can only come when the church declares that 'God is God': dies to itself and learns to listen to the action of God. When the church truly embraces the *imago Dei* (the image of God in all people) and the *missio Dei* (the mission of God in all the world) and discerns its position within the world that God made good. Karl Barth and Andrew Root are right: to be able to navigate the contours of cultural condemnation, to be able to escape the triangle of tragedy that caste, class and colour lead to, the church needs to discern the divine action that is in the world. The Christopraxis that happens through the action of the living Jesus Christ.[17] To put it more simply, when the church truly learns to see Christ present in all people and active in all the world, then it will find the light of Christ through whatever darkness it encounters. Or perhaps, put most simply over 2,000 years ago by that great Palestinian thinker, 'I am the way, the truth, and the life. No one comes to the Father but through me.'

Jesus is the way through the challenges of caste, class and colour. In each aspect of caste, class and colour, what unites us, as humans, as Christians, is our humanity. From a eucharistic prayer that I often use, 'Jesus humbled himself to share in our humanity.' Sharing in our humanity is a humbling experience, seeing the *imago Dei* in each of us beyond that which separates us. Focusing on encounter with Christ in all that we do, with the patience and humility to understand that we will get it wrong, is the foundation from which we can begin to listen to and speak to experiences of marginalization. In Christ we might truly get to grips with the multiple experiences of marginalization that are the daily reality for so many in our parishes and pews. But this will come as a challenge to an established church, because following Jesus in this way has 'confounded the mighty' for millennia.

Notes

1 The Members of the Archbishops' Anti-Racism Taskforce, 2021, *From Lament To Action*, London: Church House Publishing.

2 James H. Cone, 2010, *A Black Theology of Liberation*, 40th anniversary edn, Maryknoll, NY: Orbis Books; Anthony G. Reddie (ed.), 2012, *Black Theology*, SCM Core Text, London: SCM Press.

3 Gustavo Gutiérrez, 1991, *The God of Life*, London: SCM Press, p. 63.

4 Sathianathan Clarke, 2008, 'Subalterns, Identity Politics and Christian Theology in India', in *Christian Theology in Asia*, ed. Sebastian C. H. Kim, Cambridge and New York: Cambridge University Press, p. 272.

5 Arundhati Roy, 2020, *Azadi: Freedom, Fascism, Fiction*, A Penguin Special, London: Penguin Books, p. 81.

6 Roy, *Azadi*, p. 162.

7 Gargi Bhattacharyya et al., 2021, *Empire's Endgame: Racism and the British State*, FireWorks, London: Pluto Press, p. 118.

8 Anthony Reddie, 2022, 'Similar But Different', *Modern Church*, 22 September, https://modernchurch.org.uk/anthony-reddie-similar-but-different (accessed 22.03.2023).

9 David L. Edwards, 1998, *A Concise History of English Christianity: From Roman Britain to the Present Day*, London: Fount, p. 121.

10 Edward R. Norman, 1987, *The Victorian Christian Socialists*, Cambridge and New York: Cambridge University Press, p. 170.

11 The Archbishop of Canterbury's Commission on Urban Priority Areas, 1985, *Faith in the City: A Call for Action by Church and Nation*, London: Church House Publishing.

12 See Calvin Robinson, 2021, 'The C of E is Redefining Sin', *The Critic*, 18 May, https://thecritic.co.uk/the-c-of-e-is-redefining-sin/ (accessed 22.03.2023).

13 Hattie Williams, 2022, 'General Synod Digest: Lord Boateng Urges Church to Revisit Unfulfilled Promises on Racial Justice', *Church Times*, 18 February, https://www.churchtimes.co.uk/articles/2022/18-february/

news/uk/general-synod-digest-lord-boateng-urges-church-to-revisit-un fulfilled-promises-on-racial-justice (accessed 22.03.2023).

14 Kimberlé Crenshaw, 'Mapping the Margins: Intersectionality, Identity Politics, and Violence against Women of Color', *Stanford Law Review*, 43.6 (1991), p. 1241, https://doi.org/10.2307/1229039.

15 Kwok Pui-lan, 2021, *Postcolonial Politics and Theology: Unraveling Empire for a Global World*, Louisville, KY: Westminster John Knox Press.

16 Dorothy Sölle, 1990, *The Window of Vulnerability*, Minneapolis, MN: Fortress Press, pp. 133–41.

17 See Andrew Root, 2014, *Christopraxis: A Practical Theology of the Cross*, Minneapolis, MN: Fortress Press.

'Lifting up the lowly': Class and Leadership in Mission and Ministry

4

Consider Your Own Call: Working-Class Vocations in the Church of England

MOTHER KATHERINE LONG

Introduction

When I consider the ultimate stereotype of a Church of England vicar (an ordained deacon or priest), my mind is normally drawn to the anxious and nearly always exasperated Revd Timothy Farthing, the vicar in the 1970s BBC comedy *Dad's Army*. The Reverend Farthing is also stereotypical of his class. Indeed, he and his sidekick, Mr Maurice Yeatman the verger, are a personification of a class image of the Church of England in the 1970s (though the actual setting was of course wartime 1940s Britain). The vicar is highly strung, educated, middle class and used to being in a position of leadership alongside his hapless, less intelligent, working-class subordinate. The vicar cares for this comedic 'jobsworth' of a character, but is often exasperated by him. The verger's deference would never, ever allow him to have the audacity to address the vicar by his first name, but always as 'your Reverence'. This image has been a stalwart of British comedy. Think of the hapless, frustrated, middle-class educated Adam Smallbone with his solicitor wife in the comedy *Rev.*, or even the saintly, educated, exasperated middle-class Geraldine Granger and her working-class, stupid, bumpkin parishioners (especially Alice the verger). Comedy and literature for centuries have used this image of the middle-class vicar. This is of course deliberate, especially in the characters described above. Like many 'observational' comedy characters, it is an unconscious depiction of what the writer believes a vicar is, a portrayal of a character that elicits a subconscious universal understanding of what a character will be like for anyone who engages with the comedy, and it is this set of assumed understandings that makes the jokes funny. In other words, to make the jokes funny, both the writer and the audience (that's you and me) already have an unconscious image of what a vicar looks like, what a vicar is. Exasperated, assumed leader, educated and middle class, with their deferential, unintelligent, uneducated working-class subordinates and parishioners.

My own experiences of class and the church

I have always been a member of the Church of England and have worked in some of its most prestigious institutions. I come from a very strong working-class background, with parents who worked long and hard hours for very little money and lived in a rural working-class community (there was some mix because it was a village, but most of the villagers would be classed as 'normal' or 'ordinary', the polite code for 'working class'). When I started university and then worked for the Church of England, I found myself in a very different world, and the more prestigious the Church of England institution, the more middle class, and occasionally upper class, it became. It was a completely different culture and I had to assimilate quickly. In January 2019 I was accepted by the Church of England to train as an ordained priest (a vicar). I chose my theological college (colleges that specialize in training vicars and readers) and they sent paperwork and instructions on what I would need before I started. This included a small number of books (affordable if bought second-hand); a selection of robes, which I had to buy new and cost me just over £600 (distinctly not affordable, although I found out once I reached college that there were opportunities for second-hand robes), and of course black shoes, alongside a mountain of paperwork. While reading through the paperwork I noted how middle class the language was and how daunted I felt, despite all my assimilation from my previous experience. On reaching the college to start training, I noticed a real mix of ordinands (trainee vicars) from a variety of class backgrounds. I noted, however, that the majority were middle class and that, like the majority of the Church of England, a strong middle-class culture prevailed. This was something that some of my working-class colleagues really struggled with. It was this experience that decided the topic of my dissertation for my master's degree: I reflected that if I felt daunted by the information sent by the college and how it was written, how would someone feel who was working class and who had never been exposed to middle-class life and culture? Would it put them off? I wondered if other working-class ordinands struggled in the same way as my colleagues at college and at church if they did not 'shape shift' and assimilate to the middle-class culture. And in this consideration of my own assimilation, I reflected on my guilt, which was continually expressed in jokes about 'betraying my working-class roots' when reading the *Church Times* while drinking a cup of Earl Grey tea.

When starting to interview working-class priests and deacons about their experience, this motivation of concern about the unconscious exclusivity of the culture shifted to anger and a deep, burning belief that their voices needed to be heard; that the real impact of this assumed culture on ordinands needed to be exposed; and that church leadership, in all denominations, needed to take the class profile of its leadership more seriously and consider the impact that it is having on its church life and mission. Does the predominance of middle-class culture put a barrier on the mission of the church? Does it turn people from Jesus?

In autumn 2021, the Ministry Division of the Church of England (the group that advises and guides the Church of England on selecting and training people to be ordained as deacons and priests) began the rollout of a new selection process which seeks to remove the barriers that inhibit people from diverse backgrounds (including diverse class/socio-economic backgrounds) who feel that they have been called to be priests and deacons. The success of this new process will initially be hard to measure, because until autumn 2021 the socio-economic background of ordinands had never been recorded.[1] This was a decision taken only after a period of increasingly loud vocal activism about the church and class. For me it was also suggestive of a culture within the Church of England of 'everyone is like us'. Of course this blissful lack of awareness then fails to recognize that things that seem obvious and straightforward for some are significant hurdles to overcome for those from a different background, especially from a background where there is any kind of disadvantage. Assuming that 'everyone is like us' is a very easy trap to fall into. What was disturbing about the Ministry Division's action was just how loud the shouting had to get for any realization to occur that change might need to happen.

The research

My dissertation was a small-scale study that aimed to discover the barriers the participants had experienced in selection and training to become vicars. There were three participants who were interviewed using semi-structured interviews; that is, interviews that have questions and a basic structure, but allow the participant (the interviewee) to talk and express themselves without restriction. This allowed those being interviewed to go as in-depth as they would like, and space for their voices to be heard. The interview was broken into four sections:

- About you (the participant's background);
- Church life (prior to training);
- The selection process;
- Training.

The interviews were then analysed using a system called grounded theory. This is when you read through the interviews (written up word for word) and extract all the themes. You then use the themes as a structure to analyse the material and produce the results.

About you

In this section of the interview, I asked about their background before training. I first asked the participants to define themselves, their social class. I then asked about their housing, their parents' occupation and their own occupation prior to training, and what their life expectations were. This section was important for the understanding of class. Until a study by Savage et al. in 2013, class in academic studies had been largely defined by occupation. However, Savage's classification took into account household income, housing, cultural capital and educational background,[2] with the understanding that your definition of class was more than just your occupation. The first questions helped to build a picture of the participants.

The backgrounds of the participants were similar. They each owned their own homes but all had lived in areas of deprivation: one had lived on a council estate, another in a pit village with significant social issues relating to poverty, including literacy and obesity. This participant also experienced significant instability in their housing, having moved 10 times within the same village before training. They had all started their working lives in either manual work or service industries. All the participants had been cleaners at some point during their working lives, one had worked in catering, another as a postman. By the time they had started training, two had become managers within their organizations and one was a caretaker.

When describing their own social class, each of the participants defined their class background by their parent's occupation. Two of the participants felt that they were still working class, but one defined their present understanding of their class by their working experience (labouring) and having been brought up on a council estate, whereas the other focused more on culture and community (the poverty they experienced was normal in that community), and also defined their social class by their life expectations. One participant defined their class as technically middle class, having worked her way up from manual work (cleaning) to becoming a senior manager in a finance company. This participant felt that they were between worlds, no longer fitting their perception of working class but not feeling that they were middle class either.

The most striking responses in this section were when I asked the participants about their life expectations. None of the participants held any expectations of higher education or anticipated a professional career. One participant reflected that on asking their mother when they were young what they would do when they grew up, their mother had responded, 'Just get a job and get paid, and just pay your mortgage, that's all you need to do, and have a family.' This participant progressed at work, but this was not from ambition but to be able to provide for their family.

The school life of the participants reinforced their life expectations. One participant said that their career options were very defined: girls were taught typing so that they could do office work when they left school, with brighter girls perhaps becoming secretaries and nurses, and boys often left school to take up apprenticeships. One participant spoke about a trip organized by the school in which they were divided into two groups. The top class were taken to the local Further Education College, while the lower class were taken to a local crisp factory. The participant said that there was a sense of 'This is where you will end up.' It was during this trip that the participant was handed a form to fill in. On one side of the form there was a list of titles such as Dr and Rev. The participant reflected at the time that they would never tick one of those boxes, that they would always be 'on the other side of the line'.

All participants felt that people with working-class backgrounds rarely became priests, with two stating 'People like me don't become vicars' and another saying 'I think just that people like me, weren't vicars … I hadn't really come across many working-class priests.'

Church life prior to training

I then explored their faith and church background. I asked them about how they came to faith and when and why they started to attend church. I also wanted to know what roles they had within church and if they felt barriers against undertaking roles within the church.

None of the participants had much contact with church and the Christian faith during childhood. One started to get involved in their teenage years. This participant spoke of an awareness of God and wanting to know more, and this desire to know more drew them to their nearest church, which happened to be Church of England. At the church at this time there was a young, enthusiastic, working-class curate (trainee vicar), who the participant felt they could connect to because they were a 'real, living, breathing, bleeding person', 'unlike' people (vicars) that they met later who seemed to the participant to be 'a holier than thou, very posh, well-spoken person'. This curate, through his realness, or his class, helped nurture a seed within this participant that remained and grew until the participant was able to return to church later in their life. The other participants had a notion of faith, one through starting to ask 'What's it [life] all about?' after reading poetry during a spell of unemployment, and the other by praying that their mother would return home safe after working her shifts as a barmaid at a local working-men's club. Those participants only got involved with church later, motivated by a desire that their children should have a Christian input in their lives.

All the participants were, by the time they were selected for training, heavily involved in church life and had roles within the church. One was a church treasurer and the other two were both readers, one of whom was also a church warden. One (the reader and church warden) developed their roles in church life because they were interested and found the idea of being a church warden and a reader appealing. The other two were carefully nurtured by their parish priests, who seem to have observed the skills and potential of each of the participants and encouraged them to take up various roles within their churches.

One participant spoke of their lack of confidence, especially about reading, while another spoke of lack of confidence and feeling very self-conscious as the only working-class person in a very middle-class church. This participant, who was appointed to the church's finance committee by the parish priest, encountered prejudice because they were not a qualified accountant. They also experienced open prejudice from the young people when they led the youth group, but when the church went into interregnum (the period of time between a parish priest leaving and a new priest being appointed) this participant was increasingly looked to for leadership by their fellow readers.

All of the participants felt a sense of God calling them to ordained ministry but all, as was stated earlier, felt that people who became vicars were very different from them. Each of the participants felt that their church was supportive, but one participant experienced difficulties with their sending priest and was moved to a different church during their training. Two of the participants found that as they became more involved with worship, members of the congregation felt more able to connect and empathize with them because they were more like them: 'I think that sometimes if people aren't happy with the vicar, if you're local they can come and talk to you about it, you get them. We have this phrase in E called E people, and they'll be like, "Oh you're E people, you get it".' This participant also found that they were approached by non-Christians in the community with questions about Christianity or good and evil because the participant reflected them socially and was therefore easier to talk to.

Selection and training

Selection challenges

When someone feels that they are called by God to ordained ministry in the Church of England, they have to enter a period of discernment, in which the diocese gets to know the person (at this stage called an 'enquirer') and they both try and work out if they have been called. This process is called the Selection Process, or just Selection. When the participants were enquirers, selection involved a series of interviews with a Diocesan Director of Ordinands (DDO), who is the key person guiding the enquirer, as well as at least one interview with their bishop and a three-day assessment by a panel called the Bishop's Advisory Panel (BAP), which consists of interviews and exercises to assess if the BAP agrees with the enquirer's bishop and DDO that the enquirer is called by God to ordained ministry.

One participant experienced particular challenges with the class difference between them and their DDO and bishop. This led to assumptions being made about the future ministry of the participant. The assumption made, without consultation, was that because the participant had a working-class background they should be ministering in a working-class community. The participant also found that there was little consideration of the impact on their working life, with the DDO often turning up late for a meeting and then scheduling further meetings during the participant's working hours to make up. This led to the participant using up all their annual leave on the selection process.

One participant found BAP particularly challenging. The participant felt well prepared for the interviews and exercises but was not prepared for how they would feel: 'I went to the BAP, I felt quite out of place. All the others seemed to be well, they're all really middle-class and very well spoken and they all had jobs, such as lecturers and college tutors and things like this and lawyers and doctors, and I was a bloke who cleans toilets you know?' Another participant found the financial paperwork that needed to be completed prior to training next to impossible to complete as they felt that it was designed for traditional (nuclear) families, and it was impossible to complete if you did not fit that category (this participant was a divorcee who had remarried).

Challenges in training

None of the participants had any higher education qualifications before starting training. Two had simply finished school and started work, and the other had managed to gain some qualifications at work. All felt challenged by the academic assumptions made by their training institutions. Two of the participants had to learn to write essays, although one of the participants received support from their institution. One participant, who had undertaken some study as a Licensed Lay Minister, was expected to complete a BA in their first year and then move on and complete an MA in their second year. The participant felt that the member of staff made an assumption that the participant had the educational background required to be able to undertake such an intensive course.

One of the participants reflected that there was an assumption that there would be some financial support from their spouse or from their family, support that this participant did not have. This assumption led to the participant's anxiety concerning paying bills without this additional means of support. This participant, due to their age, also felt pressure to train part-time. This was impossible because, even though they would be training part-time, their job was too demanding; they would have to resign and the income from their spouse was not enough to support them. This was resolved by the DDO, who was able to find the funding for this participant to train full-time.

One participant needed to sell their house to pay off their debt during training, with the expectation that the profits from the house sale would cover their debt. However, the participant's house was in a low-income area and therefore its sale only generated a small profit, which did not cover the debt. This led to an investigation into the finances of the participant. For this participant this was a particularly low point during their training. The participant reflected: 'It was the only day I ever felt that if I went back to E [home village] and someone said, "I'm thinking of becoming a vicar", I'd say no, I'd say don't, if your finances aren't in order, and they won't be, you're gonna be in trouble.' When it was suggested that the participant took a break from training to cover the debt, it seemed that there was no understanding that there was a real risk of homelessness as there was nothing other than their student finance to support them.

As the participants reflected on their experience, the two participants who trained full-time had a clear sense of feeling different. One participant had grown up in an area with high levels of poverty, which was this participant's experience of 'normal'. It was only when the selection process started that the participant started to feel different, with comments such as 'We don't get many people like you' and being described as a 'pioneer'. This participant was asked how they felt about this, and their retrospective answer was 'lonely'. This continued into college, with this participant often being singled out as a 'working-class hero', which heightened the feeling of difference.

During one participant's training a study day was organized (it's not clear if it was by the students or the college) exploring the culture and issues of the local area. This included a poetry reading, where a poet put on a local accent, using local expressions in the poetry. During the reading the poet was laughing and the participant felt that the poet did not take the culture seriously. The participant frequently felt that they had to advocate for their culture and community. The participant was often asked about local expressions, and after an incident occurred concerning a student's perceptions of miners, the participant needed to explain that mining was very dangerous and miners risked their lives.

One of the participants noticed that their accent was more like the catering staff than the other students and that there was a risk of feeling as if you were the only working-class student there. However, this participant formed a friendship with another working-class student; this was mutually supportive and they found that it helped relieve a sense of isolation.

Prejudice and unconscious bias during training were felt more keenly by the two participants who trained full-time in college, and for one they were felt from the very beginning. During this participant's induction week at college they had a fire-safety talk, during which the fire officer joked, 'Don't go to [E] [the participant's home village] because they'll mug you 'cause they're all inbred.' This participant realized that it didn't occur to the fire officer that someone from E would be studying at the college or indeed be in the room. This participant also attended a lecture about ministry in difficult areas. The lecturer apologized to the participant. The participant recalled: 'The lecturer came up to me and said, "All the data I have is on E because it's pretty grim and it's too late to change it. Is it OK?" and I was like, "Yeah it's fine" and but it is that, I did feel, and it was somebody, again in that lecture there was, "E is one of the of the most deprived areas of England" and I was "Oh, I never felt deprived, but now I do".' Following the lecture an ordinand commented: 'These people from E think that they are so deprived and they're not even in the top 10.' The participant recalled thinking: 'I never thought I was deprived' and 'You're the one telling me that I am and I'm not ... like, it's not an issue to me. So it did feel like that there was a lot of that.' This participant often felt that the college community did not expect someone from a working-class background to be studying at the college, with one person from the college community saying that: 'Working-class people should just work hard and get on with it', which was met with applause from the rest of the group present. The participant found this particularly upsetting as they felt that this suggested that those from working-class backgrounds were lazy: 'I was dying to say, "Excuse me, my Mam worked three jobs and raised three kids, don't you ... don't you dare say that that my family didn't work hard and got on with it, and if you have that attitude how are you going to minister to people?"' This left the participant feeling embarrassed and that their time at college advocating that working-class people were not lazy or stupid was wasted.

This participant also found the language used around poverty in academic and church circles frustrating and inappropriate, in particular finding language such as 'escaping' areas with high levels of poverty particularly difficult. They also observed that when someone from a working-class background made an observation like this it was deemed to be a 'chip on their shoulder' rather than a genuine concern.

The other participant who was in full-time training also experienced conscious and unconscious bias; they were often mistaken for a member of the housekeeping staff and were aware that some of the younger students 'looked down on them', some doing this unconsciously, some consciously. The participant often wanted to remind these students that before college they held high-pressured, responsible jobs.

One participant, who couldn't afford to buy new shoes while they were training, wore wellington boots disguised underneath their trousers. When arriving at their placement church, they were accidently directed to the foodbank rather than the church and they had to point out that they were one of the students and were going to church. When the participant reflected on this and on many other instances during their training, they said: 'I sometimes tell myself, "Don't make a big deal of class or money or anything like that, it's not really there" and then things would happen which would make me think, "Well actually it is there."'

During one participant's training, they were taken to various locations such as boxing clubs and prisons as 'missional trips'. One missional trip was to a town that was close to the community where the participant had lived throughout their life up until training. The missional team organizing the trip would then pray for 'God to come to the town', not recognizing that God was already present there. The participant felt that this was an illustration of the church's approach to people, people who we do church with, and people we do church to.

One participant also experienced authoritarian attitudes: when announcing that the family were expecting a baby (having miscarried a previous baby), one ordinand responded, 'But you've got no money.' Reflecting on the incident the participant felt that none of their family had money, but they still loved their children.

Conclusion

From the interviews it is very evident that during their selection and training the participants found that their social class impacted significantly on their experience. Most of the experiences and prejudice were unconscious and were from a deeply ingrained attitude and expectation of who they would expect to be training as a vicar. What a vicar is expected to look like is something deeply ingrained in our society, with each of the participants stating that 'people like me don't become vicars' and 'I think just that people like me, weren't vicars', and each of the participants going into work without any expectation of a 'professional career' but a job that pays the bills and that you can get by. If you are from a working-class background, to act on a call by God to become ordained means that you are automatically jumping hurdles because you are in a new world, you have challenged an expectation that you are middle class, and suddenly you are confronted with a whole new set of hurdles. The lower hurdles are that you 'play the game' and assimilate yourself to your new class surroundings; the higher hurdles are that you do not assimilate and make yourself distinctively different from the new culture in which you find yourself, and this is the base from which a working-class ordinand has to step forward to be selected and then, if successful, train.

Throughout the selection process an enquirer is continually challenged by middle-class expectations about time availability and financial security, with the automatic assumptions that there are savings or someone you know has savings. Critically, the feeling of class difference between themselves and their interviewers (for one participant this was especially felt with their DDO and bishop), and also their fellow enquirers (one participant felt very different at their BAP from the other enquirers, who all were from professional backgrounds while the participant was a cleaner). It is this cultural difference that then continued into training, especially for the full-time participants; and it was cultural difference that was central to the experiences of the participants, frequently expressed unconsciously, often by insensitive language being used, such as 'escaping' areas that had high levels of poverty or 'bringing God to' these communities, not recognizing that God is already there and that for people living in these areas it is their home. Even using the term 'area of deprivation' can be insensitive, as those living in those communities don't necessarily feel deprived. But careless use of language can also isolate people; stating that 'We don't get many people like you' and that someone is a 'pioneer', however well intentioned, emphasizes difference.

Cultural difference was also demonstrated in attitude and expectation. This was very evident in the experience of the participant from E, a local community with a high level of poverty. This participant was not only subject to unconscious prejudice by a lecturer using the community as a case study and describing E to the participant as 'pretty grim', but also the open prejudice they experienced, with the college Fire Officer claiming that people from E were all 'inbred'. This, coupled with comments such as 'working-class people should just work hard and get on with it' or another participant being mistaken for one of the catering team, also points to the unspoken assumption that there are no working-class people in the room, and if there are, then they are domestic staff. This then shows us how deeply ingrained class prejudice is: not only are working-class people not expected to be in the room, but also it is perfectly acceptable to speak about the working class in such a derogatory and authoritarian manner. The expectation is that if a working-class person is present this language is acceptable, because they will be there in a domestic or manual capacity, thus exposing a deep-rooted class prejudice.

At the heart of the cultural difference experienced by the participants is the heavy predominance of a middle-class culture in the Church of England, with a cultural ignorance of the differences between the middle classes and working classes and the assumption that 'everyone is like us' or that 'everyone wants to be like us'. One participant clearly articulated the issue of cultural separation within the church: 'I have this big thing, that we *separate the people we do church with from the people we do church to.* And we go out and we do church to these people because they're like heathens and they don't know.' This is evidenced by the diaconal ordinal (the order of service when people are ordained deacon), where the declaration states that deacons are to: 'work with their fellow members in searching out the poor and the weak'.[3] This short statement unconsciously underlines that the church sees itself as separate from the poor, because not only are the newly ordained deacons not poor, the poor are not in immediate view, they have to be searched out. They are other.

One essential characteristic of the nature of ordained ministry is that people are called from their community to serve, and the community that they then go on to serve is the heart of their ministry.[4] Jesus was unencumbered by class prejudice and chose his followers from a wide variety of backgrounds, from fishermen (Matthew 4.18–22) to tax collectors (Matthew 10.1–4), calling them from their communities. Barrett and Harley have a vision of mission as 'inside out': community-led, embodying what is called an incarnational ministry (living out the faith and gospel teachings of Jesus in the community in a tangible and visible way), and being led by the community, rather than having people from a place of privilege come to a community to inform them of what their community and faith should look like. Listening to communities, especially communities where there are large areas of poverty, is essential in building the life of the church, and clergy need to be enabling this.[5] One of the participants, remembering their experience as a teenager, recalled how the working-class curate who so inspired them was a 'real, living, breathing, bleeding person' and it was the ability to connect and empathize because of a shared background that enabled this participant's faith to grow. Another participant found that being local gave the congregation members the ability to approach them with, 'Oh you're E people, you get it', showing how there is a real need for clergy to reflect the community they are in.

The experience of two of the participants was that clergy must carefully identify and nurture the skills and abilities of all people in their community, along the lines of Barrett and Harley's vision. This, ultimately, was what enabled the participants to follow God's call to God's ministry, and through their life experience to reach out to those who would not have had the confidence to talk to someone from a middle-class background.

Notes

1 Madeleine Davies, 2021, 'Is the C of E still a Class-Riddled Act?', *Church Times*, 25 June, https://www.churchtimes.co.uk/articles/2021/25-june/features/features/is-the-c-of-e-still-a-class-riddled-act (accessed 20.08.2022).

2 Mike Savage et al., 'A New Model of Social Class? Findings from the BBC's Great British Class Survey Experiment', *Sociology*, 47 (2) 2013, pp. 219–50; p. 224. Geoffrey Evans, 'Testing the Validity of the Goldthorpe Class Schema', *European Sociological Review*, 8 (3) 1992, pp. 211–32; p. 211.

3 Archbishops' Council, 2007, *Common Worship: Ordination Services*, London: Church House Publishing, p. 15.

4 Church of England, 2014, *Eucharistic Presidency*, London: Church House Publishing, p. 31.

5 Al Barrett and Ruth Harley, 2020, *Being Interrupted: Reimagining the Church's Mission from the Outside, In*, London: SCM Press, p. 162.

5

Resisting Coloniality: Class, Pentecostalism and Contemporary Leadership in the Church in England

DR SELINA STONE

A personal introduction

I have never been asked to write on class, despite the ways in which class has impacted on the life of my family since my grandparents arrived in Handsworth, Birmingham, from Jamaica in the early 1960s. Class differences and divisions have marked and continue to mark my life and experiences as they do for all of us – whether or not we recognize it. The reality of class as an ongoing element of life in Britain became apparent to me growing up, as I, a child of the inner-city area of Handsworth in Birmingham, became aware of the reputation of my local area as a 'ghetto'. Handsworth was an area where people from across the spectrum of ethnic difference lived together, in the kind of 'conviviality' described by Paul Gilroy, those 'processes of cohabitation and interaction that have made multiculture an ordinary feature of social life in Britain's urban areas'.[1] Many of the groups of people living in Handsworth were often united by shared experiences of migration from Britain's ex-colonies and the need to start a new life in a somewhat hostile environment. At the time of my grandparent's arrival in Handsworth, many people from across Britain's 'commonwealth' had been arriving on invitation by the government, for the primary task of working to rebuild post-war Britain. Many took on jobs along-side the working class in Britain – those of domestic workers, factory workers and labourers (it is for this reason that in Britain discussions of class must always engage with matters of race). Yet there were also some who could be considered lower middle class and even middle class, due to their jobs and access to resources. Some ran local businesses to serve the communities who needed access to the imported food and clothes that kept their cultural traditions alive. Handsworth was also a place with strong religious elements – crucial for the lives of its inhabitants. Everywhere, you could find mosques, Buddhist or Hindu temples, gurdwaras that attracted different castes, and churches that gathered Christians from different traditions.

My black Pentecostal church included people from across the class spectrum, seen most evidently in the kinds of cars lined up along the pavement in the morning before service, and the numbers of those at the bus stop or walking home afterwards. But regardless of these class differences, as a child and young person I did not consider leadership to be out of reach for me. Neither my grandparents nor my parents had been to university – my grandparents had not finished school – but they were all involved in leadership and ministry as laypeople. In Jamaica my grandparents lived and worked in rural towns. My paternal grandparents worked on a family farm and at local markets, and my maternal grandparents ran a local convenience store that turned into a local hangout in the evenings. In England, one of my grandmothers worked in domestic services in the hospital my siblings would eventually be born in. Both of my grandfathers worked in the harsh foundries of the Midlands. They were harsh not only in terms of the brutal conditions and work, but due to the racism and discrimination that they and many of their African Caribbean peers faced at every turn. At the weekends, they turned into preachers, deacons and elders, helping to lead the community of faith. Leaving school before 16 did not prevent their being respected spiritual leaders in their Pentecostal churches – in fact, their class status enabled them to better serve those in their community who came from similar backgrounds. The preaching, prayer, evangelism and pastoral care offered by those of my grandparents' generation were born out of theological reflections on their lived experience and encounters with the God who met them in the midst of numerous trials.

I write this chapter with these roots at the forefront of my mind, as well as awareness of the last five years in which I have worked within an Anglican theological college. In this context, leadership has historically belonged to white Englishmen from middle-upper classes and has only relatively recently been opened up to women. Though there have been no explicit barriers to the leadership of working-class people or people of global majority heritage, as there have been for women, the conspicuous absence of people who belong to either or both groups has been stark and highlighted by many. Various voices from within the Church of England, including most poignantly in the *Faith in the City* report of 1985, noted the need for churches to better reflect the class and racial demographics they were serving. Leadership in the Church of England was noted as too often being middle class and white, especially in contexts where the communities were working class and/or predominantly made up of those of global majority heritage. Today, conversations continue, and some innovation means that change may well be afoot in certain parts of the Church. But overall, the Church's leadership continues to be predominantly made up of middle-class people of all ethnic groups in a country where increasing numbers of people find themselves among the lower classes.

This chapter is about class and leadership in the Church in England today but it begins by exploring history. Though there can be some reluctance to look back at British history – for we find much horror there amidst the claims of glory – it is there that we will find clues to the patterns and disorders that manifest in the present. We will therefore look back at colonial notions of Christian leadership, which centred on the 'the middle-upper-class English "Christian" gentleman' who would lead the 'heathens' to salvation while exploiting people and place. This, I believe, still haunts some aspects of Christian imagination regarding leadership, especially in the historic denominations and those within the evangelical traditions, including some Pentecostals. In contrast, we will consider how Pentecostalism (as distinct from the charismatic movement among historic denominations) is a historic movement at the margins, which has centred the leadership of those from working-class backgrounds, women and people of global majority heritage. Christian leadership in England may be revived by moving beyond the classism often exemplified by historic denominations (most notably the Church of England) and learning from the leadership of 'the least of these', exemplified in this case by early Pentecostals.

Class, race and colonial Christian leadership

There are many historical vantage points from which we could explore the questions of class and Christian leadership. But since, as I have asserted, race should be explored as interlinked with class in Britain, it is important to find a point at which this connection is clear. I will therefore look back to the context of Christian leadership in the era of the British empire and specifically the era of enslavement in British colonies. This empire was understood to be a Christian empire, rooted in the ambitions of an English elite, beliefs about English exceptionalism, and Christian doctrines that supported white supremacist logics. The Christianizing of European ambitions to dominate the world is a clear example of the Church, her traditions and the Scriptures being co-opted for political and economic gain. But in this chapter, I want to focus on how the English Christian imagination regarding leadership has historically been formed by classist and racist notions of personhood. In other words, we must take a critical approach to reflecting on what we consider to be models of good Christian leadership, in the light of how these ideas have been distorted by racist, classist and capitalist ideologies rooted in the colonial period.

Analyses of Christian colonialism and the enslavement of Africans are often explored as a social justice issue, from the perspective of race and racism. The problem of race is clearly seen in the particular dehumanization of Africans and the destruction and exploitation of entire people groups across Asia and the Americas. Countless pieces of evidence have been presented of the racist attitudes held regarding indigenous peoples, some of the earliest examples being in the papal bulls that gave sanction to colonial savagery by the European powers in what is known as the 'Doctrine of (Christian) Discovery':

> We weighing all and singular the premises with due meditation, and noting that since we had formerly by other letters of ours granted among other things free and ample faculty to the aforesaid King Alfonso – to invade, search out, capture, vanquish, and subdue all Saracens and pagans whatsoever, and other enemies of Christ wheresoever placed, and the kingdoms, dukedoms, principalities, dominions, possessions, and all movable and immovable goods whatsoever held and possessed by them and to reduce their persons to perpetual slavery, and to apply and appropriate to himself and his successors the kingdoms, dukedoms, counties, principalities, dominions, possessions, and goods, and to convert them to his and their use and profit – by having secured the said faculty, the said King Alfonso, or, by his authority, the aforesaid infante, justly and lawfully has acquired and possessed, and doth possess, these islands, lands, harbors, and seas, and they do of right belong and pertain to the said King Alfonso and his successors.[2]

The English eventually followed the path that the Portuguese had forged with the help of the Pope, taking over parts of the Caribbean, America, Africa and South Asia from the early 1600s. By this time Queen Elizabeth I was the reigning English monarch, and while embedding a clear identity for the Church of England would be one of her main objectives, so would establishing the British empire – in fact the two could be argued to have worked hand in hand. Church of England priests and the Church as a whole participated in and benefitted economically from colonialism and the enslavement of Africans. This has rightfully been denounced from all quarters.

However, the problem of colonialism and enslavement was not simply a matter of social inequity due to race; it also amounted to an economic exploitation – something that comes very close to what we think of today as 'class'.

The European trade and enslavement of an estimated 10–12 million African people between the fifteenth and nineteenth centuries – most of whom were enslaved by the British – is often considered to be the ultimate fruit of racism. The logic is that Europeans were driven to enslave Africans because of their hatred for Africans, who they viewed as subhuman and sought to exploit and oppress. Yet in *Capitalism and Slavery*,[3] Eric Williams, a Trinidadian historian and politician, offers a nuanced analysis of colonialism and the enslavement of Africans that recognizes racism and the impact of capitalism as a motivator. Rather than viewing racism as the core motivation for slavery, he argues instead that it was the demands of capitalism, which required cheap labour and a constant workforce:

> Slavery was an economic institution of the first importance. It had been the basis of Greek economy and had built up the Roman Empire. In modern times it provided the sugar for the tea and the coffee cups of the Western world. It produced the cotton to serve as a base for modern capitalism. It made the American South and the Caribbean islands. Seen in historical perspective, it forms a part of that general picture of the harsh treatment of the underprivileged classes.[4]

Africans were enslaved en-masse not, in Williams' estimation, because of anti-black racism (even though this helped to justify it) but due to the effectiveness of Africans as labourers in contrast to the indigenous people of the Americas, who died off quickly due to disease. This determination to find free or cheap and effective labourers crossed racial boundaries. Interestingly, in Williams' history he notes that indigenous labourers were not immediately replaced by Africans but by white indentured servants and then by increasing numbers of people who had been convicted of crimes in England:

Some were indentured servants, so called because, before departure from the homeland, they had signed a contract, indented by law, binding them to service for a stipulated time in return for their passage. Still others, known as 'redemptioners,' arranged with the captain of the ship to pay for their passage on arrival or within a specified time thereafter; if they did not, they were sold by the captain to the highest bidder. Others were convicts, sent out by the deliberate policy of the home government, to serve for a specified period.[5]

The point of this is not to argue that poor white people were treated as badly as Africans or that they shared the same fate. The circumstances in which Africans were kidnapped and sold into slavery and transported to the Americas in conditions that many did not survive cannot be compared to that of English people who were given a limited sentence of hard labour. Nor is Williams suggesting that racism did not play a role in slavery – the dehumanization of Africans who could be legally owned as property was rooted in racism, while white indentured servants were still recognized as human because of their whiteness. However, he seeks to prove that capitalist economics was the core driver in the fate of the poor white servant *and* the enslaved African – and therefore, historically speaking, class and race can be seen as intertwined forms of injustice and oppression.

In this colonial context then, the white and wealthy Church and its leaders are seen as complicit not only in racialized oppression of Africans, but a broader class-based exploitation. The man in charge of the white servant and the black slave in the colonies was the English Christian gentleman (and often his wife). These figures were seen to represent Christian mission, through which they might develop African men into a kind of 'civilized' state that was not only white English but was 'gentlemanly'. 'Christian' ministry in the colonies had a particular appeal for the Evangelical Christian man in particular, as I have argued elsewhere in discussion with the work of Catherine Hall:

For Hall, Christian mission in the colonies was not simply a project which would appeal to all Christians in Britain who wanted to take part in the civilising of global populations; it was an endeavour which had particular relevance for the identity of a Christian Englishman. Christian missionary work is presented here as an avenue for success and power for men who sought to embody the best of what it meant to be English: not only to be the white male hero but the white male *saviour*, tasked with Christianising the 'heathen' and the 'savage'.[6]

Leadership in such a time and space is driven by capitalist logics and legitimized by classism and racism. The white servant and the black slave, and the white owner or 'leader', are all viewed as being in their appropriate places. Their places are appropriate when judged by a kind of natural law – which from ancient times suggested that some people were simply born to serve or be enslaved while others were born to lead. But this 'natural order' was also spiritualized, with colonial theology arguing, for example, that Africans were enslaved as a fulfilment of Noah's curse of his son Ham. The mistreatment of white indentured servants could easily be argued as due to divine providence, and the hard labour of those convicted of crimes be seen as divine judgement for wrongdoing. Above both of these groups deemed subhuman and immoral would stand the 'purity' of the wealthy Englishman and his wife whose actual godlessness and savagery was sanctioned, according to Williams, by England's capitalist ambitions.

Pentecostalism: a model of anti-classism

Since, as we have seen, capitalist ambitions have historically resulted in the poverty of so many people, the dehumanization of Africans as well as the exploitation of indigenous lands and peoples globally, class and race are inextricably inter-linked. This link remains when discussing Christian leadership in England, a discussion that cannot be had without reckoning with the history of the established Church of England, which is embedded within the history of British colonialism. There were of course individuals who worked towards the abolition of the slave trade, but they were not, as it were, within the structure of the Church, which as a whole did not oppose it.[7] The Church of England has historically been a religious institution organized and led predominantly by a particular group of people – the middle-upper-class Englishman – with particular ideas about possession and command. That is not to say that every priest or leader in the Church wants to adopt or has adopted this model, but the culture and agenda of the Church has for the most part been (and some would argue continues to be) driven by such people. However, colonial models of Christian leadership, in which all must conform to or submit to the 'white (English) middle-upper-class gentleman' in order to be recognized and accepted, stifle the possibility of the Church and its mission. As difference is eradicated or consumed, rather than valued and given room to flourish, the body suffers – not only that of individuals but the Church as a whole. But this is not the only historic model of Christian leadership. In order to ask what Christian leadership might look like beyond this classist and racist model, we will turn now to Pentecostalism.

Pentecostalism can – and I would say should – be understood as a movement among the 'least of these'. The story of Pentecostalism testifies to this fact. The key figures of the movement, and the majority of those who were part of it, belonged to working or lower classes. The movement is often located as beginning at a revival among a small group of African American believers who gathered on Azusa Street in Los Angeles, in a poor part of the city. William Seymour, who would lead the Azusa Street congregation, was the son of enslaved Africans and worked as a waiter before then becoming a preacher and pastor. The Azusa Street gatherings drew many people who knew poverty and social exclusion first hand. Elsewhere around the world, stories of Pentecostalism include similar revivals taking place among Dalit communities in India, which challenged unjust orders within the Church in particular:

> Dalits themselves are also known to have experienced a level of liberation through Pentecostal faith from the 1920s on-

wards. In a context where Syrian migrants in India were considered to be superior to the indigenous groups, the church congregation embodies a different model of relationship. The Indian peasants were brought into 'mutual cooperation and shared table fellowship' with Syrian Christians in the Pentecostal churches.[8] This was uncommon, and in many congregations it was previously the norm for them to be discriminated against and treated as second-class citizens.[9]

This position among the poorest has continued all the way through the movement's development until the present day. While Pentecostalism belongs to a more middle-class demographic in the UK today, it has historically thrived among working-class communities of all ethnic groups. The main groups that contributed to the early movement in the UK were white working-class communities in the north of England and in Wales, and African Caribbeans coming to rebuild Britain from 1948 onwards. Globally, Pentecostalism continues to grow exponentially in parts of Latin America and Africa that deal with significant levels of poverty, while Christianity declines in the so-called 'developed world'.

When it comes to leadership in British Pentecostal churches, several important notes should be made in relation to class. Historically, as I have mentioned, the majority of Pentecostal churches belonged to working- and lower-class migrants, with some middle-class people involved as members and leaders. This meant that leadership often included those who did not have formal education or a certain set of managerial skills but were recognized as having the necessary character, spirituality and skills for leading others. This might include oratory skills, pastoral gifts or what is often described as 'having the anointing' – a recognition by the community that they have the capacity for enabling those they lead to encounter God. The preference for these measures of good leadership as opposed to a focus on intellectual abilities or critical reasoning and analysis has often been spoken of as a form of 'anti-intellectualism' within the movement. There is some legitimacy to this claim for those Pentecostals who are concerned that intellectual study might undermine faith or one's 'anointing' to lead others. However, from the earliest days Pentecostals understood the importance of reasoning and engaging with the Bible in an intellectual way, even if that did not mean taking particularly critical approaches. In Bible colleges, Pentecostals in Britain have often studied the Bible and its contexts and Christian theology, but always in a manner that was deeply connected to encounter with God (spirituality) and the practice of leadership. What should be taken from Pentecostal preferences in relation to leadership is that they are led by the needs of those they serve, not a professional ideal that has been imported from elsewhere. The movement began among poor Americans of all ethnic groups, was led by an African American man who descended from enslaved Africans, and gave room to women's ministry and leadership. It stands in stark contrast to the colonial ministry of the white middle-upper-class English gentleman who stands alone at the apex of a hierarchy that holds the poor (and especially poor Black people) at the bottom.

Leadership within the Pentecostal imagination, which I was raised in, was understood as being accessible to all people because God is the one who calls and equips for leadership by the Holy Spirit, and the Holy Spirit is neither classist nor racist nor sexist. Within the Pentecostal mind, God may call, equip and give gifts to whoever God wills in order to bring about God's purposes. This includes children, women, those without much formal education, migrants and those living with disabilities. Within this movement God not only includes those labelled 'working class', 'poor' or 'marginalized' but centres them in the story of God's renewal of the world. Pentecostals have learnt to be content with the mysterious ways of God that appear to be 'foolishness' in the eyes of the world.

While Pentecostalism is diverse and in no way immune from the seduction of classist, racist or sexist models of leadership, its earliest roots call all Christians regardless of tradition to a different way of being. At Azusa Street we see Christian leadership in the Spirit and outside the colonial frame, where the overlooked are recognized and celebrated as equal, where the ministry of women is welcomed, and the spiritual gifts of children enrich the community. In the long revival services, we see a laying down of the idol of productivity that undermines the life of God, and the taking up of the call to rest in God and with one other. In the humble beginnings of this movement, we find the logic of the kingdom at work, in which a person sows seeds and goes to sleep and entrusts the harvest to God and the rhythms God has set into the natural order. Who could have imagined that a group of working-class black people praying to encounter the Spirit would ignite a spiritual movement that would continue to reverberate around the world today, and that the son of ex-slaves would be its leader?

If we pay attention to the story of Pentecost it becomes easy to imagine. In Acts 2 we read that the disciples had been gathered waiting for the Spirit promised to them by Jesus, and then she arrives like a wind, appearing like tongues of fire on the heads of those who were gathered. They start speaking supernaturally in other languages, and crowds of people testify that they can hear the good work of God being talked about in their native languages. We celebrate the moment as a sign of the inclusive work of the Spirit in terms of culture and ethnicity, but what attention do we pay to the other aspects of the people in the story? Some of the disciples who receive the Spirit would fit into the categories we would call 'working class' – Simon Peter, Andrew, James and John are fishermen. And of those who happened to pass by the upper room – a random place in their local community – and heard of the good news in their own languages: how many of them would have been wealthy, powerful, or representatives of the elite? This entire scene, spoken of by many as the birth of the Church, does not take place among the wealthy, the formally educated or the political or religious elite, but most likely among the everyday people on their way to the market or home from work.

Conclusion

Christian leadership within Pentecostal spaces that imbibe the spirit of the early movement should be recognized as a prophetic sign of the Spirit's calling and equipping of all people regardless of class, race or gender. And yet it is also true that a movement that had such politically subversive roots has tended to professionalize in ways that undermine this heritage. With the increased interest in training and education that tends to follow a traditional western model of 'mastery', Pentecostals run the risk of losing what it is that makes the movement such a gift to the Church and the world. Denominations restrict women's ministry in ways that did not happen among the early Pentecostals. And the racial divides are most striking when we consider how the peoples of the world were initially gathered together under one roof at Azusa Street. It is Pentecostalism's historic openness to any person that the Spirit empowered, being called to lead, preach or give a prophetic message, that shames tendencies only to entrust these contributions to those from middle- or upper-class backgrounds, and especially white men. This is the prophetic witness that Pentecostalism brings to conversations about leadership in the Church and the world.

I end this chapter with a Pentecostal hope that the same spirit that has revived the Church in so many places and times, may again revive the Church in England. The revival I hope for does not revolve around spiritual gifts such as speaking in tongues or prophetic utterances, but in the arrival of the Spirit who anointed Jesus to set the oppressed free. In this revival, a reordering of power might occur, casting down whatever opposes the work of God who seeks to lift up the lowly, not only in history but in our present day and time.

Notes

1 Paul Gilroy, 2004, *Postcolonial Melancholia*, New York: Columbia University Press, p. 12.

2 Papal Bull, *Dum Diversas*, 1452.

3 Eric Williams, 1994, *Capitalism and Slavery*, Chapel Hill/London: University of North Carolina Press.

4 Williams, *Capitalism and Slavery*, p. 5.

5 Williams, *Capitalism and Slavery*, p. 9.

6 Selina Stone, 'Sisters in the Hostile Environment', *Black Theology: An International Journal* (forthcoming, 2023); emphasis original.

7 William Wilberforce was a politician who converted to Christianity in his 20s and went on to lead a parliamentary fight to overturn the slave trade in Britain's colonies, alongside Granville Sharp (scholar and abolitionist), Thomas Clarke (an ordained deacon turned abolitionist) and others known as the 'Clapham Sect'.

8 T. S. Samuel Kutty, 2000, *The Place and Contribution of Dalits in Select Pentecostal Churches in Central Kerala from 1922–1972*, Delhi: ISPCK.

9 Selina Stone, 'Pentecostal Power: Discipleship as Political Engagement', *Journal of the European Pentecostal Theological Association*, 38:1 (2018), p. 30.

SECTION 3

'Casting down the mighty from their thrones': Class, Solidarity and the Struggle for the Common Good

6

'Bullshit Jobs': The Church and the Precariat

REVD DR SALLY MANN

As people who hope for the Church's relevance in British culture, I invite you to consider two recent shifts within our class system. One is the emergence of a new class, the Precariat. The other is what is happening to middle-class employment and the increase of 'bullshit jobs'.[1] I believe it's vital to understand some of the shifting patterns of class. I intend to bring these into a conversation with some of the ways we think about church life and leadership, and then, after some chastening thoughts, to end on a hopeful note. I write as a sociologist, activist and ordained minister. I will be putting my own experiences and ministerial context into conversation with sociology and theology. I'm from an East End working-class background; the fourth of six generations to live in the same four streets in East Ham, Newham. Class matters to me: academically, experientially, vocationally and even spiritually. I am convinced that if we don't pay attention to changes in the structures and realities of class, we risk speaking in tropes and stoking social resentment. But if we know what is happening, we may identify opportunities for our churches to become 'contrast communities' embodying hope to those caught in the worst repercussions of the changing class landscape in Britain today.

The rise of the Precariat

The working class has been eviscerated. Globalization, post-industrialization and what has been innocuously termed the 'flexible labour market' have done away with it. The massive transformation of class in Britain can be traced back to the neo-liberal politics of the 1980s. A raft of economic policies prioritized the needs of a free market and dismantled the social institutions that reined in its reach, weakening labour's bargaining power to the extent that much of the progress on workers' rights made in the 1950s was effectively undone. The working class in Britain would not be the same again. The reshaping of class within Britain was hastened by the acceleration of globalization, which Polanyi described as 'The Great Transformation' of work (1944). The British socio-economist Guy Standing agrees but offers the prediction that a 'second great transformation' is afoot, one marked by the end of state welfare capitalism and the rise of a new class in Britain – 'The Precariat'.[2] These are the new working class, defined by unstable labour arrangements, lack of identity and erosion of rights. They are the growing ranks of precarious workers, positioned just above the unemployed and the most heavily excluded, who Standing calls the 'Detached'.

Precariat work demands geographic and occupational mobility making life inherently unstable. There are multiple insecurities. First, the precariat experience insecure employment; working for agencies or juggling several 'gig' jobs in a lifetime of 'career-less' occupations. Then there are unpredictable hours and insecure incomes. Precariat jobs are often offered with zero-hour contracts, while others are forced to take sessional work with little opportunity to plan ahead or budget. Far too many experience perpetual in-work poverty. Finally, precariat employment undermines any status or identity the former working class could achieve through belonging to an occupational community where they could rise through the ranks.

The rise of the Precariat has shifted the risks and fluctuations in demand from employers on to an army of their more casually employed workers. It's a good time to be a chief executive in

Britain. The 'flexible labour market' has resulted in CEO wages rising exponentially, bouncing back rapidly from the effects of the Covid pandemic. According to Deloitte's 2022 AGM season report, the overall pay for chief executives in the FTSE 100 has reached a median average of £3.6 million, fully regaining the pre-pandemic levels within one year. In 2022 the median employee to FTSE 100 chief executive pay ratio was 1:81, compared with 1:59 in 2020. But it's a terrible time to be starting out in the employment market, even as a graduate. Precariat employment is most sharply increasing among the 'professions' such as teaching and health care. The Resolution Foundation suggests that disproportionately high numbers of young people returning to work are doing so on an insecure basis and that in 2019–20 around one in ten (9.7%) of the UK's working population could be considered precarious workers.

We knew the extent of inequalities born from changing patterns in employment back in 2016, when the then Prime Minister, Theresa May, issued the Taylor Review.[3] This was to be a landmark document. It concluded that 'Insecure and exploitative work is bad for health and wellbeing and generates a cost for society' and that the quality of experience in the workplace impacted citizenship. It made radical and wide-ranging recommendations, which included the need to focus on the *quality* of job creation, and the need for government ambition to ensure that 'all work is fair and decent with scope for fulfilment and development'. The Taylor Review made 53 recommendations for change, of which 51 were accepted by the then government and written up into a 'Good Work Plan' in December 2018. But a recent report by the TUC found that the number of British workers in precarious employment has increased from 3.2 million, when the Taylor Review was published, to 3.6 million in 2021. Their analysis suggests that most of the recommendations have still not been implemented. The Precariat are the fastest-growing class in Britain.

The increase in precariat and other low-pay jobs is having a far-reaching impact on tax and welfare budgets. Precarious employment raises the tax burden as increasing numbers of working families fall below the breadline and require financial support. Universal Credit can be claimed by those in low-paid employment. The total number of people on Universal Credit has decreased but a greater proportion of them are employed, some 2.3 million claimants by March 2022.[4] At the same time, 47% of all families claiming housing benefit in the private rented sector are in work. Low pay has resulted in UK private landlords receiving £9.3 billion in housing benefits payments, twice as much as a decade ago.[5] While the poor are often represented as being a burden on taxpayers, it's those who pay low wages and charge high rents who are driving up welfare budgets.

There is unprecedented movement at either end of the social ladder in the UK. At one end, a tiny elite hold an escalating proportion of national wealth. In 2019 the UK's six richest people held a combined fortune of £39.4 billion, as much as the combined assets of the poorest 13.2 million Brits.[6] At the bottom of the ladder, a growing proportion of Britons are falling below the poverty line. According to the Resolution Foundation, the cost-of-living crisis will push 1.3 million people, including half a million children, below the poverty line.[7] The tapering, elongating ladder of British class is the result of policy decisions in employment, tax, housing and welfare. The changes at one end of the ladder are reliant on what is happening at the other.

My borough, Newham, has a 37% poverty rate, which is the second highest rate in London. It has one of the highest proportions of low earners in England, with more than a third of workers paid less than the real Living Wage, which was £10.20 per hour for workers in London when the data was compiled. The latest figures from the Office for National Statistics show 33.8% of jobs in Newham pay less than the real Living Wage – around 23,000 workers in total. The working lives of the Precariat are often a mishmash of temporary or zero-hour contracts: delivery drivers, cleaners, retail staff and care workers, sometimes underemployed, sometimes overworked. They cannot easily budget or access mortgages or credit, and perpetually 'rob Peter to pay Paul'. This is East Ham through and through. Here, low wages are exacerbated by high rents, resulting in overcrowding and a good deal of informal, and often abusive, tenancy agreements. As work dries up, they face months of low or no pay, often living on informal handouts, overdrafts, gambling and payday loans, and dreams of winning the lottery to put an end to the stress of in-work poverty.

Guy Standing titled his analysis *The Precariat: The New Dangerous Class*. The danger is not only to the individual lives of those caught in precarity, but Standing predicts that there is a social cost: the rise of popularism and far-right politics, bred by working-class discontent; growing social unrest, riots and protests; and perhaps a third hopeful outcome – the possibility of new grass-roots-led organization for social change. We have surely witnessed the first two of Standing's predictions; are we as communities of faith perhaps well placed to enable the third? I will return to this later, but there is a further shift in how Britons experience class which, when understood, may offer opportunities for meaningful missional engagement. This time it is the salariat experience, which sociology may help us to interrogate and discover the existential threat to those working in our economy's burgeoning bureaucracy.

'Bullshit jobs'

It is not only the newly emerging Precariat who are feeling the strain of changes to employment in Britain. The middle class are experiencing a plight that might not be immediately noticeable but holds profound existential threat. Professor David Graeber, an anthropologist from the London School of Economics, argues that there are millions of the middle class, from clerical workers and administrators to consultants and corporate lawyers, who are toiling away in meaningless, unnecessary jobs, and they know it. This is the rise of 'bullshit jobs'. Graeber says that as labour-intensive jobs became mechanized, modern workers might have been freed from the suffocating 40-hour working week. Instead, Western cultures have invented a whole raft of futile occupations that are professionally unsatisfying and spiritually empty. He notes the paradox whereby some low-paid jobs are hard and have terrible work conditions but are often very useful: 'the more useful the work is, the less they pay you.' 'Bullshit jobs' are often highly respected and pay well but are completely pointless; the people doing them are aware of this. The pandemic forced a temporary national awareness of our reliance on the essential work of retailers, delivery drivers and carers. As much as they were cheered during the pandemic, the reality is that these workers continue to be hit hardest by the low-pay and cost-of-living crises. Meanwhile, those facing endless pointless tasks, long hours and little satisfaction, increasingly resent the taxes they pay, which they see as funding those escaping dismal work lives. Tax avoidance is therefore not only permissible but those whose corporations pay the least are lauded as the most successful. Resentment and alienation between the classes hastens the end of the welfare state, which has been a strong feature of liberal democracies, and undermines the social fabric of British society.

I have explored here that two of the most populous classes in Britain face existential threats to their well-being: the precarious lives of the working poor humiliate and enrage; the pointless work of many in the middle class drains and builds resentment. Where does the Church come into this equation? What has Christianity to say in this context?

Jesus and precariat experience

I imagine that Jesus of Nazareth might relate to the oppression of the Precariat today. As a 'peasant artisan carpenter' his class was often pitied in agrarian societies. The original biblical word to describe Jesus' occupation suggests that his family had lost ownership of their land at some point and now sold their labour.[8] Land was the dominant means to generate wealth and power in the pre-capitalist biblical world. The control of land was complex in Jesus' day, with local, religious and empire elites compounding the oppression of both peasants and landless workers.[9] A landless, jobbing carpenter of the time would have found insufficient work in the tiny village of Nazareth, with an estimated population of perhaps as few as 400 people. Instead, Jesus would most likely have walked down the hill from Nazareth to work in the regional capital city Sepphoris, just four miles away and visible from its outlying, much poorer, hillside villages. Sepphoris was moneyed in comparison. It had private bathhouses fed by aqueducts, an armoury and paved roads. Historically, we know that many of the buildings in Sepphoris had been razed to the ground by the Roman Empire as punishment for an uprising that sacked the armoury. This would have happened in Jesus' childhood. The empire trampled out such insurgence with mass executions and by destroying many of the city's buildings. Jesus might well have walked to work six days a week, in a kind of gig economy of his day. He surely noticed that the aqueducts flowed in one direction – taking water from the hills of Galilee into the wealthy villas of Sepphoris with their private bathhouses. It is interesting that while all four Gospels tell us that Jesus is from Nazareth, not one mentions Sepphoris. Incarnation happens in an innocuous place of no prestige, through a man whose adult life had been one of labouring under an oppressive regime, building homes that he could not afford to live in before walking uphill home. Reading the Bible with an awareness of the class structures and struggles of ancient societies is just a starting point. The class lens also requires us to interrogate the biases brought to hermeneutics through the privileged class positions of main-stream biblical interpreters, and indeed our own starting points. In a similar way that discourses around 'race' have challenged naïve hermeneutics that attempt 'colour-blind' exegesis, it is well overdue that Western interpretation should also look at class privilege as skewing our reading of Scripture. How many Western readings assume that we should primarily relate to the slave nation of Israel in the Exodus when we might more profit-ably learn from seeing ourselves reflected in Pharoah?

Once we grasp social class as one of our most significant ways of being in the world, affecting all that we do, including our biblical interpretation, we gain an unexpected resource. As we frankly embrace our own social class advantages and disadvantages – including our pain that humans should be divided in this way – the anguish and the grandeur of the biblical record dawns upon us with previously unexperienced power.[10]

Theologies of class as a justice issue

My sociological insights and contextual theology strongly suggest that class inequality is best appreciated as an issue of *justice*. As such, the state of the Precariat and those trapped in 'bullshit jobs' are not just descriptions of contemporary British life but are clearly sinful. Class inequalities in the UK are an affront to the values of the kingdom of God and the biblical vision of *shalom*. In seeking a theology of class I find it best to begin with a version of Gerhard Lenski's deceptively simple question, 'Who Gets What and Why?'[11] This approach focuses on class as a social relation based on production. The exploitation inherent in this relationship creates groups who partake differentially in the goods, services and ideas within society. The 'why' question encourages us to interrogate the persistence of inequalities and the roles of ideology and social institutions, such as the Church, in maintaining and advancing the interests of one group over another. At the heart of a justice reading of class is the appreciation that the advantages of the elite are directly in relation to the exploitation of classes beneath them. It is possible to begin a theology of class on this premise, as Joerg Rieger does, for example.[12] Without this, mainstream church conversations limit discussions of class to matters of culture, identity and inclusion. I find the realities of class inequality offer a more fundamental theological challenge and a place for local congregations to be at the cutting edge of manifesting the good news of the kingdom of God in this regard. I will conclude my discussion with some practical examples of this from my own community, but will briefly explore characteristics of the theological thinking fundamental to this approach.

First, theology has enormous resources to understand labour exploitation as *structural sin*. Liberation theologies offer theoretical resources for this exploration. Models of salvation that take class seriously identify 'binding the strong man'[13] of class oppression as part of the good news that Jesus brings. Economic exploitation is one of the 'powers that be' that the Church is called to 'name, unmask and engage with'.[14]

Second, the biblical vision of *shalom* has resources to imagine redeemed social organizations of power. There is much to say here. I have found great resources in Robert Linthicum's biblicism and practical application.[15] Theological to the core, Linthicum brings the sweep of the Bible to understanding political, economic and religious life and how these become structured around a community's power dynamics. He sets out a biblical mandate for relational power and offers a thoroughly Christian framework for consciously organizing power on behalf of God's vision of *shalom*. This reading takes class seriously and is predicated on a contemporary reading of God's preferential option for the poor that avoids patronizing and disempowering those in poor communities.

Third, a theology of 'class as a justice issue' will inevitably shape missiology. Joining the mission of God in the world involves interrupting systems of injustice. This is not only a matter for protest but for the type of proclamation that comes from attempts to shape 'contrast communities' informed by a biblical vision of *shalom*. This is costly. Ash Barker explores this in the call to 'make poverty personal' and take the poor as seriously as the Bible does.[16]

Opportunities and challenges for the Church in an age of precariat and 'bullshit jobs'

Much of church life in the UK is fashioned by middle-class assumptions. Within my own denominational stream there is a definitive way of 'doing church' based upon attending services and programmes. When we ask about church affiliation, we mean whether a person attends these in prescribed ways at set times. Some churches have moved to multi-service patterns to allow for more variation in work patterns or other commitments, but usually there is the assumption that 'membership' is characterized by being reliably present and available to participate in the programmes, which are an addition to a person's 'regular' life. This excludes the Precariat. 'Doing church' through programmes may not be enough to address the emerging middle class's needs for a spiritual reality that reaches the parts of them seeking something more profound and radical from their faith.

The class-based presuppositions governing how to 'do church' also shape how to 'lead church'. Can many church leaders truly identify with the Precariat? It seems very unlikely that many leaders from white British denominations have any direct experience of the levels of precarity and insecurity faced by the fastest-growing class in Britain today. The work patterns of professional clergy mimic those of Standing's 'salariat class'. Some assume 'jobs for life' in their theologies of vocation and many have the practical advantages of secure housing provided with their work. Many clergy can build careers; they may even have formal structures to check and assess their professional ministerial development. However demanding ministry is, it provides far more in terms of purpose and meaning than 'bullshit jobs' (I'll leave others to argue whether the inner workings of denominations have fallen prey to the tendency to produce these within their structures). Are clergy from mainstream Euro-tribal denominations, to borrow Al Roxburgh's term, insulated from the realities of both precariat and middle-class working lives today? If this is the case, they can expect some resentment, or at best a sense of disconnect, from those trapped in jobs that offer few of the pragmatic or spiritual benefits of church ministry.

However, is there a sense in which the leaders of faith communities might be precisely in the right context to organize for broader social change? This was the third and only positive outcome Standing predicted in the rise of the Precariat. Injustice would be countered by grass-roots organization and radical, structural economic change. Christian communities have the added advantage of the wealth of scriptural visions of *shalom*, deep resources to reimagine economic justice. These visions can, and have, provided ways for communities to think through how to realize the biblical vision of *shalom* in new social arrangements that shape more than how we gather for worship. As we understand the pressures of both the Precariat and those in 'bullshit jobs', there is a spiritual opportunity to connect with their needs. Church communities can articulate the struggles and hopes for identity and meaning and offer opportunities to work for justice at the local level – whether by providing volunteering opportunities or through setting up social enterprises and charities that model other ways to value and define work.

There are many ways to earth this. We might think through pathways to ministry that are more inclusive. Technological innovation to make in-person gathering one of many ways to connect as a congregation is also clearly important. Certainly, rethinking ecclesiology is at the crux of all of this. However, since I am convinced that global problems are best addressed in the communities most sharply affected by them, I seek my answers in attempts to discern what the Spirit is up to in the local. Here are a few snippets of how I see my own faith community innovating and experimenting in ways of being church that address class realities in the UK. In my own community, Bonny Downs in East Ham, I have experienced church as a place for soft power. Living among the Precariat in Newham, practices have emerged that, on reflection, have helped us to address some of the changes in class and, more than this, to be a community that articulates the call for justice and change.

I end with these snippets from my own community:

- For the past three decades we have prioritized community organization as a missional practice, setting up a grass-roots charity that provides a wealth of well-being projects and today employs 40 local people on permanent contracts, paid at the London Living Wage or above (www.bonnydowns. org).
- Our church plans to pull down its existing building and, rather than build a worship venue, has designed an 'Urban Abbey', a co-living enterprise where missional couples will live alongside eight single people transitioning from homelessness. There is more space given to 'tables than stages' in our expression of church. There is space for communal meals,

a roof terrace and food growing. These are mustard-seed expressions of the type of community we believe reflects the *kenarchy* of God (the rule of love).

- We are a small church with few salaried members. We set aside a communal hardship fund between us to provide interest-free loans of up to £200 so that we have direct access to emergency funds as members who are committed to each other's well-being.

- The charity we helped form now provides CAP money courses and a debt advice centre. Our experiences of being an emergency food provider during Covid led to setting up a Family Hub where those with 'no recourse to public funding' find mutual support and cook and eat together, with advocates on hand and a church pastor to offer chaplaincy.

- We are a Baptist Church and have shifted to a flatter pattern of church leadership. Bi-vocationality is a norm for us. Four ministers, appointed by the church members, divide one stipend between them. This has released time and energy to pursue diverse employment opportunities. One of our ministers set up a gardening cooperative, which trains and employs people experiencing homelessness. Others work for the charity we helped set up and in community organization roles.

- We are moving to gatherings that happen in different 'sacred spaces'. Our main Sunday gathering happens in a community garden. Keeping some church activities 'blended' by livestreaming and using online platforms means we are less reliant on gathering in person, and those working can tune in later.

- We hold 'generosity meals' (www.commonchange.org) where we gather and decide how to spend our collections for local needs.

This is some of my experience in my local church. It is not beyond any congregation to innovate and experiment in ways that address the needs of the emerging class system. There are so many ways that faith communities are relevant in articulating the call for employment justice and organizing with those trapped in precarious or 'bullshit jobs'. We can join existing local campaigning groups like Citizens or, as we have done, innovate and experiment locally for the common good.

Conclusion

These personal reflections are offered in the hope of encouraging a missiology that is properly alert to the changes in British class systems. My community has found that a Christian vision of *shalom* has not only informed our diagnosis of what is wrong with how things are, but also provides the spiritual resources to sustain our attempts to model alternatives. Seeking *shalom* has become our way of discipleship.

How might these reflections be received? Ched Myers, in offering a political and liberative reading of Mark's Gospel, predicts three possibilities:

> [Mark's Gospel] is a story by, about, and for those committed to God's work of justice, compassion, and liberation in the world. To modern theologians, like the Pharisees, Mark offers no 'signs from heaven' (Mark 8.11f.). To scholars who, like the chief priests, refuse to ideologically commit themselves, he offers no answer (Mark 11.30–33). But to those willing to raise the wrath of the empire, Mark offers a way of discipleship (8.34ff.).[17]

Notes

1 David Graeber, 2018, *Bullshit Jobs: A Theory*, London: Simon & Schuster.

2 Guy Standing, 2011, *The Precariat: The New Dangerous Class*, London: Bloomsbury Press.

3 Matthew Taylor, 'Employment Practices in the Modern Economy', commissioned by the Prime Minister on 1 October 2016, https://www.gov.uk/government/groups/employment-practices-in-the-modern-economy (accessed 22.03.2023).

4 'Universal Credit statistics, 29 April 2013 to 14 April 2022', *Gov.uk*, https://www.gov.uk/government/statistics/universal-credit-stat

istics-29-april-2013-to-14-april-2022/universal-credit-statistics-29-april-2013-to-14-april-2022 (accessed 22.03.2023).

5 The National Housing Federation, https://www.housing.org.uk/. The NHF chief executive David Orr said: 'It is madness to spend £9bn of taxpayers' money lining the pockets of private landlords rather than investing in affordable homes.'

6 The Equality Trust, https://equalitytrust.org.uk/, is a website bringing evidence of the widening inequality gap in the UK.

7 Torsten Bell, chief executive of the Resolution Foundation, https://www.resolutionfoundation.org/.

8 Geza Vermes, 1973, *Jesus the Jew*, New York: Macmillan. Jesus' class is a contested debate. Jesus' poverty and marginalization are most strongly supported in Luke's Gospel and explored in the following commentaries: Joachim Jeremias, 1969, *Jerusalem in the Time of Jesus*, London: SCM Press, p. 304; Richard Horsley, 1989, *The Liberation of Christmas: The Infancy Narratives in Social Context*, New York: Crossroad, pp. 102–6; and David A. Fiensy, 1991, *The Social History of Palestine in the Herodian Period: The Land is Mine*, Studies in the Bible and Early Christianity 20, Lewiston/Queenston/Lampeter: Edwin Mellen.

9 Norman K. Gottwald, 'Social Class as an Analytic and Hermeneutical Category in Biblical Studies', *Journal of Biblical Literature*, 112, 1 (Spring 1993), pp. 3–22.

10 Gottwald, 'Social Class", p. 22.

11 Gerhard Lenski, 1984, *Power and Privilege: A Theory of Social Stratification*, Chapel Hill, NC: University of North Carolina Press, title of chapter 1.

12 Joerg Rieger (ed.), 2013, *Religion, Theology, and Class: Fresh Engagements after Long Silence*, New York: Palgrave Macmillan.

13 Ched Myers, 1988, *Binding the Strong Man: A Political Reading of Mark's Story of Jesus*, Maryknoll, NY: Orbis Books.

14 Walter Wink's trilogy 'Naming, Unmasking and Engaging the Powers', is summed up in Walter Wink, 2000, *The Powers That Be: Theology for a New Millennium*, new edition, New York: Bantam Doubleday Dell.

15 Robert Linthicum, 2003, *Transforming Power: Biblical Strategies for Making a Difference in Your Community*, London: IVP.

16 Ash Barker, 2009, *Make Poverty Personal: Taking the Poor as Seriously as the Bible Does*, Grand Rapids, MI: Baker Academic.

17 Myers, *Binding the Strong Man*.

7

Recovering the Radical: Lessons of Class Solidarity through a Case Study from the Iona Community

VICTORIA TURNER

I sometimes feel that the church's profound ignorance of the life and story of the poor is as incredible as it would have been, if for example, God the Father, seeking to help the human race, had decided to become incarnate – as a dog.[1]

This quote is from John Harvey, Leader of the Iona Community 1988–95. John spent his ministry in council estates, and between 1966 and 1968 he worked with the Gorbals Group Ministry, which overtly sought to show the gospel message through political and social action among the poor.[2]

Many who know the Iona Community today would most likely explain their work by describing their inclusive and globally inclined worship resources from the Wild Goose Resource Group, their retreats on the Island of Iona on the west coast of Scotland, perhaps their Celtic spirituality and connection to the land (George MacLeod famously called Iona a 'thin place' between heaven and earth), maybe (though less likely) their commitment to non-violence and nuclear disarmament. What is ironically less well-known or remembered popularly, is the foundational reason for the Community's existence – the mission to the working classes.

Researching this integral aspect of their work has been transformational for me. Class was not something I thought about while I was growing up, or a topic that me and my friends would ever discuss. I spent my school and my taught university years working to fit in with those from a different class from me. During my undergraduate years in Bristol, I had a part-time job to a) afford rent and b) afford the aesthetic and lifestyle of term time while friends would fly to Bali for their summer holidays. Part of my obliviousness to class struggles, however, was my ambiguous relationship with class, or my in-betweenness. I grew up on a council estate in Cardiff but both my parents worked and I went to the church school rather than the failing local high school. Most of my school friends lived in a different area from me. I have written elsewhere about how my obliviousness to my own class location stunted me from being aware of, or in solidarity with, others who were marginalized by our white, masculine, upper-class, heterosexual and cisgendered power structures.[3] But I was not exposed to a different narrative – a narrative of struggle – until I delved into researching the Iona Community. In many ways, as Joerg Rieger has recently commented, this uprising in thinking about class is new.[4] It has not been explored well in academic theology nor academia more widely. But that does not necessarily mean that the work has not been going on at the grass roots. Academia is gatekept and controlled by those of privilege, so only a narrative that is interesting to those in this circle is prioritized and advanced.[5] The history of the Iona Community, however, has pushed me to ask hard questions about my own upbringing: who belonged in my church and whose voices do I listen to and respect? The Community's tireless work of fighting the class struggle for generations holds so much wisdom and resilience for those of us ready to delve into it today. In this chapter I will take a critical look at the Iona community as a case study, reflecting on 'where the radical has gone' in the relationships between churches and working-class communities.

Introducing the founder of the Iona Community: George MacLeod

George MacLeod, born on 17 June 1895, entered into an aristocratic family. His father, Jack MacLeod, was a successful accountant and devoted Conservative Party supporter, and his mother, Edith, came from the Fielden family, who owned one of the largest cotton manufacturers in the world.[6] George grew up in Park Circus Place, Glasgow, in a comfortable situation, with the house served by a cook, maid and nanny. After attending an Edinburgh prep school, he went to Winchester College and then studied Law at Oriel College, Oxford.

George became conscious of his class privilege when serving during the First World War. His father Jack was the recruitment officer for the 11th and 1/8th Argyll and Sutherland Highlanders, and George (an Oxford student) entered this battalion as an officer. His faith was very important during this time. He reveals in a letter to his mother in the July of 1917:

> I have heard it said that a man comes out of this war with a very real religion or no religion at all ... personally, I think any man who sees this war, must come out with a very real religion or cut his throat! I can't see how it's bearable to the 'no religion at all class.'[7]

This was most likely MacLeod's first close contact with the religiosity, or irreligiosity, of working-class men. Diffusive Christianity, being an imbedded, cultural, comforting type of Christianity, showed itself in the urban working class through the 'phenomenal popularity of hymn singing',[8] occasional prayer and the willingness to attend services run by the YMCA or the 'padres'.[9] The sense of community among fellow men seemed to alleviate the horrors of the war, alongside discussions of 'revolutions' after the war providing some hope.[10] The mixture of Scottish culture, Presbyterian legacies and the diversity of class representation would have been a strange mix to George, who would have spent most of his formative years surrounded by an upper-class Anglican education system, yet had a strong familial legacy of service in the Church of Scotland.[11]

After the war George studied for ministry with the Church of Scotland at the University of Edinburgh. Following a few apprenticeships in Edinburgh, MacLeod accepted a call to be the minister of Govan Parish Church. This was a very deprived area where 80% of the population was unemployed. The manse where George lived was a flat attached to the Pearce Institute, which formed part of the church. The full exposure of living in working-class areas, rather than merely visiting them as in the case of his parishes in Edinburgh, was a culture shock for the privileged MacLeod. In a letter, Tubby Clayton, with whom George had previously worked in Toc H, shared that 'I am glad you have left Govan [...] had you gone on in the Pearce Institute you would have been worn out in a few years whereas Iona will enable you to be mature without becoming old.'[12] To live at a distance from the working classes but to be involved in advocacy for them and training others to serve with them would have been a more gentle role for MacLeod in his 40s. Tubby's concerns about George struggling in Govan were not unfounded. In 1933 George had taken a trip to Palestine and Egypt with his father in an attempt to recover from his 'hopeless depression'.[13]

Forming community

The missionary impetus of the project was clearly set out in George's early explanations of the Iona Community (or as it was referred to in the earliest years, the brotherhood). The Iona Community consisted of half craftsmen and half ministers-in-training for the Church of Scotland, who lived on Iona during the summers, in basic conditions, to rebuild the Abbey.[14] The off-season saw the trainee ministers serve their apprenticeship in disadvantaged industrial parishes.[15] Ralph Morton, who for a time was MacLeods' Deputy Leader, explained in 1953 that: 'It was the recognition of the needs of the parish, particularly in the industrial areas, that led to the founding of The Iona Community.'[16] The aim of the Iona Community was to create missionaries to serve at home.

By 1940 the mission had extended from the Island of Iona into the parishes, with Iona men serving in ten churches. Most of these parishes had two Iona men serving alongside the already appointed minister. The men would specialize in activities such as youth work, reducing drunkenness, increasing membership with parish visitations, or working with the Community to improve the area. The distance between the training on Iona and the field in the working-class parishes exemplifies the class divide between the Church of Scotland and its urban areas. The idea that privileged graduates needed a programme that placed them in a difficult and strange situation (with employed, skilled craftsmen) to prepare them for ministry in industrial areas is reflective of George's struggle with his exposure to Govan. Furthering this, the placement of men in teams in these parishes suggests not only that the Church was lacking numbers in these areas, but that the context was deemed too difficult for one man to face on his own. The use of these structures to make these working-class areas appear accessible seems to feed a narrative that they are impenetrable, dangerous, alien and risky.

Dangerous narratives

Dangerous narratives surrounding the poor are familiar territory for us today in Britain. Owen Jones' popular work has revealed how mainline propaganda vilifies and scapegoats the working class, or 'chavs', to continue their neglect by the austerity-happy Conservative government.[17] John Harvey also commented in the 1980s how the limited decisions of the poor are judged by the upper classes, who did not have the context to understand why a tumble dryer was a necessary purchase – the person had no green space to hang out laundry, nor could they be assured it would be there when they returned.[18] Harvey also upholds a definition of poverty that highlights the inability to be a full part of the 'community' and points towards the distance between classes being key to this rift.[19] Joerg Rieger, in his most recent work, upholds the importance of community and solidarity and connects the topic of class to capitalist exploitation and the increasingly reducing voice and power in society of the working person or the person with the inability to work. In his discussion on the misguided use of the word 'classism' he writes:

> The term suggests that the problem of class has to do with class stereotypes rather than relationships of extraction or exploitation. As a result, the use of the term classism tends to imply that the problem can be overcome by doing away with class stereotypes, neglecting relationships of power or exploitation. This is often how class is addressed in religious communities, which seek to 'celebrate diversity' and consider their mission accomplished when millionaires and homeless people share the same pews.[20]

This pushes against alternative ideas that seek to 'help' the poor fit into the system of exploitation via changing their culture and moulding them into the middle classes who had apparently found God. It also argues against those who think alleviating poverty needs charity rather than political action.[21] Theology that seeks to enter the working-class culture without an aim of liberative justice but rather with an apolitical acceptance of them and an inclusion into their structures, and without the aim of transforming these structures, are further fetishizing the working class and ridiculing their exploited positionality. As members of the Iona Community spent more time among the working classes on the mainland, the community quickly turned towards political action and away from the missionary saviour idea embedded in MacLeod's early assumptions.

Youth

Gradually, the mission of the Iona Community became less focused on the men on the Island and more visible through its work on the mainland. This changed what it meant to be part of the Iona Community. Membership moved away from being a separated brotherhood with an agenda to 'save' working-class communities, and towards a community made up of a diversity of members working to transform the society and culture of Scotland and beyond. Interestingly, it was the vision of young people that pushed the Iona Community out of its exclusive identity into an inclusive, fluid movement.

This engagement with young people was unexpected by some early Community members. Duncan Finlayson recollected to Anne Muir, who completed an oral research project about the early Community, that when George was asked in the first few years if he was planning to involve young people, he commented: 'If the community gets drawn aside into getting involved with young people, it'll be a complete disaster.'[22] Three years later, he and John Summers (a youth worker and Iona Community member) decided that youth groups needed a Christian renewal, and on 4 January 1942 they together started a youth group in Canongate, Edinburgh, called the Christian Workers' League.[23] The boys in the club were encouraged to think and govern themselves, which led them to go beyond the structure of the Iona Community and include girls just three months after the club opened – 30 years before the Community would make this decision.[24] Paulo Freire, the revolutionary educationalist, wrote that 'sectarianism, fed by fanaticism, is always castrating. Radicalization, nourished by a critical spirit, is always creative.'[25] The organic involvement of the young members in their own decision-making allowed them to understand their own liberation and deconstruct the oppressive structures in their own community. Freire writes about how this organic involvement creates a liberative educational structure, given that: 'Self-deprecation is another characteristic of the oppressed, which derives from their internalisation of the opinion the oppressors hold of them.'[26] The young people were encouraged to discern and act in their own community, building not only skills and confidence, but tangibly changing their own context for the better themselves.

By 1946, MacLeod wrote in the Community magazine, The Coracle, that he wished Iona to become 'a Mecca of Scottish youth in summer-time'.[27] Upwards of 600 young people visited the island every year during the summer months in the late 1940s and 50s. Not all of those who made the journey to the summer camps belonged to the Church of Scotland, or to Christianity at all for that matter. A youth worker in charge of the camps in the 1950s (himself only 23 at the time) remembers MacLeod insisting that 65% of the young people needed to come from disadvantaged backgrounds, making the group of them extremely diverse.[28] The success of these camps inspired the gift annually of a £20,000 grant, received for several years, donated by Sir James and Lady Gwendolyn Lithgow in 1943 for the purpose of youth work. The aim of the Iona Youth Trust established by this grant was to 'further the work of the Church of Scotland among young people "in accordance with the principles of the Iona Community"'.[29]

The 'central experiment' of the Youth Trust was the Community House, originally envisaged as a 'Youth House', purchased at 214 Clyde Street, Glasgow.[30] Ian Renton, a Community member, painted the scene to Anne Muir: 'You had criminals, borstal boys, Divinity students, students from the university, people off the street for lunch. Everyone.'[31]

The Community House sought to explore faith, politics and real-world issues through debate, fellowship and creativity. Aimed at young adolescents who had left school, the centre provided a space to rekindle hope and find purpose for those in depressing contexts through discussion, study, Bible study and action.[32] Class enrolment for courses such as 'mission preparation, divine healing, political and industrial, drama, film direction, international and country dancing, youth leadership and meaning of the faith' was 2,464 for 1951–3.[33]

Exploring the contention with a political mission

Although immensely popular with young people, the Community House's relationship with the larger Iona Community, the staff's relationship with Community members and Trustees, and the Iona Community's relationship with the Church of Scotland caused confusion and tension.[34]

Politics were also important for the Trust's chief benefactor, but for him it was to be kept separate from his faith. Sir James

Lithgow was a successful industrialist, inheriting his father's shipbuilding company in Glasgow and later owning multiple shipbuilding and steelmaking companies with his brother Henry Lithgow. The brothers were brought up devout Presbyterians and donated a vast amount of money to the Church of Scotland in 1936 after pledging the profits from the sale of James Dunlop & Co.[35] They were also generous benefactors to their industrial community, evidenced by the town of Port Glasgow awarding Sir James their first honorary citizenship.[36] However, in the era of Red Clydeside and the captivation of Communism for many impoverished industrialists, James Lithgow publicly criticized organized labour.[37] Organized trade unions were a threat to his 'rationalistic' approach towards his industrial empire. These unions were also a breeding ground for more general Communist politics and ideas. In the late 1940s and early 1950s, Scotland constituted one of the CPGB's (Communist Party of Great Britain's) largest 'districts', with a formal membership of around 6,000, organized in 305 branches.

Communism was taken by some to be a very serious threat to Christian life in Scotland and beyond. Young people were considered especially susceptible to the 'idealism' present in the Communist message.[38] In the Trustee meeting of 8 May 1950, the Board, along with the Lithgows, studied a letter from James Lithgow in which he stated his concern about the political nature of the Iona Youth Trust's Community House, seeing that membership to the Iona Community seemed to imply also membership of the Socialist party. Lithgow resigned from the Trustee board (though his wife Gwendolyn stayed) on 4 September 1950. In his resignation letter he outlined that:

> The lines of approach suggested [in Community House] permit participation in Party politics by the instructors. This does not accord with my views as I am totally opposed to associating religious instruction with the doctrines of a political party.[39]

He acknowledged that he was not an expert in these matters and that it would be unfair for a granter of the Trust to overly influence its direction. Community House and the Community carried on with their political agenda.

This fear from the Church towards the political activism of young people has not diminished. In a press release just after the launch of my edited book *Young, Woke and Christian: Words from a Missing Generation*, a journalist asked if the volume should be called 'Young, Woke and Labour' and a panellist compared the young people's strong commitment to justice to Putin's extreme totalitarian rule.[40] The fallacy of neutrality that surrounds the institutional Church, in the attempt to keep the powerful happy and the elite position of the Church secure in society, alienates and belittles the motivation of young people to bring justice as disciples of Christ's kingdom.

Mission to the working class in the late 1970s–90s.

The last warden of Community House, Campbell Robertson, came to be known as the authority on homeless support as Community House moved away from being a location for youth education.[41] The year 1977 saw many ends for the Community, including the death of Ralph Morton, John Summers the pioneer of the Christian Workers' League and the summer camps, and also the demise and abandonment of Community House.[42]

Witness to young people in Scotland's parishes, however, continued with the work of John Bell and Graham Maule, who both moved to the Community from the Church of Scotland as youth workers to expand their scope, namely reaching non-churched young people.[43] Ron Ferguson, who was Leader of the community from 1982 to 1988, points to Kathy and Ian Galloway, the joint wardens of the Iona Abbey and their 'gifts in leading worship and in imaginative education' that attracted young adults to the Island.[44] This, however, overlooks the important work on the mainland that spread the work and facilitated young people travelling to the Island. The most ambitious project of Bell and Maule, yet one that ties most closely to the enduring legacy of the Iona Community, began in 1982 and was called 'Columban Houses'. Bell and Maule sought to overcome the class divide in society by having teams of young people train on Iona to live in council estates in community, while on welfare, to help others in difficult positions as one of them. They could then bring disadvantaged young people to Iona, alongside helping them day to day to get into work and education and off drugs.[45] John Bell recalled in an interview the backlash this project received from many. The young people would 'pool' their benefits to live in a community but for some it was too counter-cultural and 'taking advantage' of the government.[46] The anti-capitalist stance of living without regard to economic worth and alongside those who had fallen through the cracks of Thatcher's years of austerity, individualization and the planned breakdown of the solidarity of the working classes was completely against the status quo, and for John Bell, one of his proudest projects.[47]

The end of the 1980s is where this history of the mission of the Iona Community ends. The work of Bell and Maule ended a long legacy of Community-funded work on the mainland. Of course, ministry in parishes and collective advocacy work continued, but the restructuring of the organization (inspired by international members), away from the re-envisioning and re-animation of the Church of Scotland (and other churches through ecumenical members) in Scotland towards peace-building and justice overseas and in politics, shows a dramatic shift in the model of the Community.

Why has this happened? Reflection

I find it can often be tempting to look back on history either with rose-tinted glasses or with contact lenses made of flames – only painting a fully good or fully bad picture. The closest, most realistic interpretation of the past we can get is one that understands that people in the past were as complicated as we are today, and we do not fully understand their complications just as we do not fully understand our own. This usually means that reflection lands somewhere in the middle, honouring the motivations and aspirations of those in the past but also using the gift of hindsight to see where they missed the mark.

For the Iona Community, their method of reaching the working class undoubtedly changed. By the 1980s, grass-roots work with working-class people increasingly became an off-hand, 'shushed about' side project of the Community that was too controversial even to talk about. On the other hand, we could say that the work of the 1970s and 80s was much more authentic than MacLeod's original experiment, which was rife with paternalism and the Victorian romanticism of the 'deserving' working class, and where education that fitted people into an acceptable model was advanced rather than a revolutionary, actively political model of justice. MacLeod's fear of difference was emphasized with the enduring brotherhood and retreats on Iona to 're-train' for the challenging context. Bell and Maule, however, were based in Glasgow and lived alongside working-class people in the same conditions. Robertson, even further, washed the feet of the homeless community. This was not about uplifting the working classes into the educated middle classes with an ulterior motive of pushing them away from Communism. This was mission with, and alongside, the working classes. The 'Last of the Month' worship services organized by Bell and Maule were led by young people, to inspire each other. The divide between minister and working-class recipient began to blur with this method, which started to overcome the paternalistic middle-class saviour complex we often see.

The contexts are also telling. After the First World War, the working classes, although feeling the effects of the economic depression, had a different identity following their service in the war. Thatcher's 1980s demonized the working classes and their trades. Post-protests and strikes, this created an environment of hopelessness, worthlessness and frustration that we still see today. Working-class people often do not have pride in their trade as they once did because governments laughed at their working lifestyles and the communities that sustained them. From the 1980s, an underclass developed, those forgotten in society and demonized in order to take the attention for their deprivation away from governments. It was not celebrated, or sexy, to communicate with the unworthy poor in our later (and today's) contexts. After the 1980s, the youth work of the Iona Community increasingly became concentrated on 'Community kids', who were the children of the middle-class Community members, and since 2010 no more youth workers have been employed by the Community. Today there is a Young Adults group that connects students and young Community members and is run by the young people themselves. Reaching people who are not like you, however (as I hope we have learnt from this chapter), takes dedication, getting your hands dirty and real investment. If we are only *protesting for*, and not *protesting with* the working classes, if we are only *doing to* and not *organizing with* the working classes, we are slipping back into paternalistic patterns.

As Charles Taylor commented in his *The Malaise of Modernity*, an individualistic, capital-driven society where people are 'enclosed in their own hearts' is one where 'few will want to participate in self-government', and even if they did, 'the individual citizen is left alone in the face of the vast bureaucratic state and feels, correctly, powerless. This demotivates the citizen even further.'[48] Additionally, as Joerg Rieger has argued, the labour rights of working people have become less democratic and more removed, creating a cold, unjust yet seemingly immovable system of exploitation.[49] Our work to overcome structures of class injustice seems more necessary than ever in a society whose government believes that plunging people into coldness, hunger and pollution is a non-negotiable normality, that people can simply find a better job if they want a different life. The drastic distance between those who govern and those who supply and labour is unimaginable. John Harvey plays with the metaphor of Jesus coming down as a dog to illustrate the blindness of the Church to the plight of the poor. Today, it feels more like the Church is Larry the cat, resident of Downing Street. The Church cannot but see current injustices – its members everywhere are hungry, cold and struggling – but instead of mobilizing, it decides to lie down, comfortable and warm, and bask in its glory of tradition.[50]

Notes

1 J. Harvey, 2008, *Bridging the Gap: Has the Church Failed the Poor?*, Glasgow: Wild Goose Resource Group (reprint from Edinburgh: Saint Andrew Press, 1987), p. 40.

2 For the work of the Gorbals Group, see A. Forsyth, 2019, 'Theology and Practice of Mission in Mid-Twentieth-Century Scotland', in D. Fergusson and M. Elliott (eds), *The History of Scottish Theology, vol.III: The Long Twentieth Century*, Oxford: Oxford University Press, pp. 242–58.

3 See V. A. Turner, 'Interrogating Whiteness through the Lens of Class in Britain: Empire, Entitlement and Exceptionalism', *Practical Theology*, 15, 1–2 (2022), pp. 107–19.

4 Tripp Fuller, 'Joerg Rieger: Divine Justice and our Ultimate Concern' on *HomeBrewed Christianity* podcast.

5 See E. Parker, 2022, *Trust in Theological Education: Deconstructing 'Trustworthiness' for a Pedagogy of Liberation*, London: SCM Press.

6 R. Ferguson, 1990, *George MacLeod: The Founder of the Iona Community*, London: Collins, pp. 18–19.

7 G. MacLeod, 'Letter to Mother', 25/07/1917, Letters from the Western Front to his family, 11 June 1917–28 Nov 1919 (Acc.9084/37).

8 Michael Snape, 2005, *God and the British Soldier: Religion and the British Army in the First and Second World Wars*, Christianity and Society in the Modern World, Abingdon: Routledge, p. 53.

9 Michael Snape, 2005, *The Redcoat and Religion: The Forgotten History of the British Soldier from the Age of Marlborough to the Eve of the First World War*, Abingdon: Taylor and Francis, p. 177.

10 G. MacLeod, 'Letter to Mother,' 20/06/1917 (Acc.9084/37).

11 His grandfather Norman MacLeod was the most famous Church of Scotland minister of the Victorian period and was remembered for his dedication to the working class. This legacy was eclipsed by the political leanings of his father Jack.

12 P. B. Clayton, 'Letter to G. MacLeod 20/10/1938', *MacLeod General Correspondence to 1939* (Acc.9084/60).

13 G. MacLeod, 1934, *Govan Calling: Sermons and Addresses Broadcast and Otherwise*, London: Methuen, p. 100.

14 It is a commonly asserted that MacLeod brought unemployed craftsmen into the project, but this was not the case. The 'basic' living conditions were contested by Henry Cockburn, who visited the Community in their second year. He wrote in the *Scottish Daily Express*: 'the "hut" contains a big living room, kitchen quarters, 26 sleeping cubicles, and a range of bathrooms, well-supplied with hot and cold water [...] I chuckled over Dr MacLeod's description of the house as offering "neither extra comforts nor affected austerity."' H. Cockburn,

'Today on Iona: Abbey Builders', *Scottish Daily Express*, 12/06/1936 (Acc.9084/129). It's quite telling of MacLeod's confidence, or perhaps humour, that he kept this newspaper cutting in his curated collection.

15 R. Ferguson, 1988, *Chasing the Wild Goose: The Iona Community*, London: Fount Paperbacks, p. 66.

16 R. Morton, 'In Parishes in Scotland', *The Coracle*, 24 (December 1953), p. 15.

17 O. Jones, 2020, *Chavs: The Demonization of the Working Class*, third edition, London: Verso Books. A good friend, Sharaiz Chaudhry, pointed out how White the analysis of the working class is in this book, which is important to bear in mind when consulting it.

18 Harvey, *Bridging the Gap*, p. 44.

19 Harvey, *Bridging the Gap*, p. 43.

20 J. Rieger, 2022, *Theology in the Capitalocene: Ecology, Identity, Class and Solidarity*, Minneapolis, MN: Fortress Press, p. 116.

21 See C. R. Pemberton, 2020, *Bread of Life in Broken Britain: Food Banks, Faith and Neoliberalism*, London: SCM Press.

22 Anne Muir, 2011, *Outside of the Safe Place: An Oral History of the Early Years of the Iona Community*, Glasgow: Wild Goose Publications, p. 44.

23 The Christian Workers' League was inspired by the Roman Catholic Young Christian Workers, part of the international *Jeunes Ouvrières Chrétiennes* network, which sought to expose young Catholic Christians to social injustices and mobilize them for action. *Youth File* (NLS, Acc.9084/288).

24 J. Summers, 'Christian Workers League,' *The Coracle*, 10 (March 1943), pp. 25–8.

25 P. Freire, 2017, *Pedagogy of the Oppressed*, London: Penguin Classics, p. 11.

26 Freire, *Pedagogy of the Oppressed*, p. 37.

27 G. MacLeod, 'The Iona Youth Trust', *The Coracle*, 13 (September 1946), pp. 22–4; p. 24.

28 Interview, Zoom, 16.10.2020.

29 Ferguson, *George MacLeod*, pp. 197–8.

30 G. MacLeod, 'Community House, 214 Clyde Street, Glasgow', *The Coracle*, 23 (November 1953), p. 20.

31 Muir, *Outside of the Safe Place*, p. 67.

32 T. Ralph Morton, *The Iona Community: Personal Impressions of the Early Years* (Edinburgh: St Andrew Press, 1977), p. 71.

33 MacLeod, 'Community House', p. 23.

34 Morton, *The Iona Community*, pp. 78–80.

35 A. Slaven, 'Lithgow Family (per c.1870–1952)', *Oxford Dictionary of National Biography*, posted 25.05.2006, https://www-oxforddnb-com.ezproxy.is.ed.ac.uk/view/10.1093/ref:odnb/9780198614128.001.

0001/odnb-9780198614128-e-51878?rskey=qelMjO&result=1#odnb-9780198614128-e-51878-headword-3 (accessed 26.10.2020).

36 Slaven, 'Lithgow Family (per c.1870–1952)'.

37 'James Lithgow', *Grace's Guide to British Industrial History*, https://www.gracesguide.co.uk/James_Lithgow (accessed 22.03.2023).

38 E. W. McFarland and R. J. Johnston, 'The Church of Scotland's Special Commission on Communism, 1949–1954: Tackling "Christianity's Most Serious Competitor"', *Contemporary British History*, 23, 3 (2009), pp. 337–61.

39 Trustee Meeting Minutes (4 September 1950) in *Iona Youth Trust Minutes 1943–46*, NLS (Acc.9084/642).

40 Ruth Peacock, 2022, 'We're Young, Woke and Christian: Hear our Voices', *Religion Media Centre*, 23 March, https://religionmediacentre.org.uk/news/were-young-woke-and-christian-hear-our-voices/ (accessed 22.03.2023).

41 Ferguson, *Chasing the Wild Goose*, p. 145.

42 Ferguson, *Chasing the Wild Goose*, p. 145.

43 E. Brink, 'For Whom the Bell Toils: An interview with John Bell of the Iona Community', *Reformed Worship*, https://www.reformedworship.org/article/march-1993/whom-bell-toils-interview-john-bell-iona-community (accessed 22.03.2023).

44 Ferguson, *Chasing the Wild Goose*, p. 149.

45 Ferguson, *Chasing the Wild Goose*, pp. 160–1.

46 Interview with John Bell, Glasgow, 25.09.2020.

47 The idea is not dissimilar to the early work of Lex Miller in the late 1940s. See K. Jacobs and S. P. Walker, 'Accounting and Accountability in the Iona Community', *Accounting, Auditing & Accountability Journal*, 17, 3 (2004), pp. 361–81.

48 C. Taylor, 1991, *The Malaise of Modernity*, Toronto: House of Anansi Press Publications, pp. 9–10.

49 Rieger, *Theology in the Capitalocene*, pp. 110–11.

50 Thank you, Phillipa Osei, for this witty metaphor.

8

Class in the Classroom: Social Class and Theological Education

DR EVE PARKER

There is no iniquity so vile, no crime, however monstrous, that the Church has not blessed and sanctified if perpetrated in the interests of the rich and powerful.[1]

'Knowledge is Power' may strike us as a naïve Victorian slogan, but it was embraced passionately by generations of working-class radicals who were denied both.[2]

In 2018 the Bishop of Burnley called on the Church of England to expand its priesthood and give focus to the working class, stating that the procedures for the selecting of ordinands, 'hugely favour eloquence and education and confidence, over authenticity and evangelistic gifts and genuine vocation'.[3] When middle-class bishops profess a need to reach out to the working class, such 'missional' desire cannot be trusted unless the bishop also seeks to profess a demand for class justice in the face of class struggle. The difficulty, of course, is that the middle- and upper-class clerics live in isolation from such struggle. While on the surface expressions of desire for more working-class representation are welcome, they should be approached with caution if the desire for societal transform-ation for the working-class condition is not met with the same hopeful intentions of action in the face of inequality. To suggest that the working class are not educated, or that education is an elitist weapon to be held only by the ruling classes, serves only to further segregate and polarize the working class. Class identification that reduces the working class to being 'uneducated' risks erasing systemic class difference that is brought about by economic and social privilege. Class operates in a way that produces and distributes unequal value to individuals and groups, and education, as we shall come to discuss, is one of the greatest weapons of the working class that can be used as a means of challenging such privileges. Defining class is extremely complex and often contested; for Pierre Bourdieu, for example, class structure 'encompasses the entirety of the occupational division of labour'[4] and is determined by 'capital' – 'the set of actually usable resources and powers',[5] including economic, social, cultural and symbolic capital. Katie Beswick further notes that class is 'inherently intersectional, always entangled with injustices related to race, gender, sexuality and disability, to the extent that it is difficult to understand the lived experiences and stigmas produced by distinct identity positions as separate from class'.[6] This chapter will give particular attention to the notion of social class, as outlined by Bourdieu, in order to address the working-class experience within the wider class hierarchy in Britain, with particular reference to working-class experience in theological education.

In Britain, the working class continue to be the majority,[7] and this fact is not to be taken lightly when the Church has a vested interest in reaching out to the people at a time when numbers of those professing faith in the Church have, according to the 2022 census, reached an all-time low. The concern, of course, is the intentions behind the 'reaching out'. Britain is also a nation that is segregated by class: the plight of the poor is increasing at unprecedented levels, the greed of the wealthy elites is not only tolerated but also enabled through seemingly democratic processes whereby those elites are repeatedly elected to power to rule over the masses. The general population can then appear passive to class inequality. This became apparent when Boris Johnson won the general election in 2019, despite using class slurs to attack the working class, stating, 'Working-class men are likely to be drunk, criminal, aimless and feckless and hopeless.'[8] Class struggle has become a notion that is mocked and manipulated by the media.[9] The dominant political parties are guilty of sidelining and silencing the trade unions, by condemning the industrial action of the working masses who call for fair pay and safe working conditions. It is vital to ask, therefore, in the midst of such social realities and class struggle: what does it mean to educate for class consciousness and why is this relevant to the role and purpose of theological education today?

My intention in this chapter is to consider the ways in which *theological* education can enable class consciousness. Some might argue that this is not the role of theological education, but if the role and purpose of theological education is, as Rowan Williams argues, 'learning more about the world that faith creates, or the world that faith trains you to inhabit', class consciousness must surely be included in this. Williams goes on to say that:

> To do theology is, in some ways, to be taken back to that moment of bewilderment about the newness or the distinctiveness or the strangeness of being in this new Christian framework. So theological education is familiarizing yourself with how people have found their way around that landscape with the perspectives they've occupied and then learning to pitch your own tent, as one might say, in that territory.[10]

Class is therefore a central notion to be grappled with within the landscape of theological education, especially as more working-class students enter the classroom. I will therefore consider how, in the words of bell hooks, theological education can 'teach to transgress' as a means of challenging class inequality and educating those in formational training to help bring about social change. I will engage with the lived experiences of working-class students in theological education institutes in the UK – with a particular focus on those in formational training for ministry. Next, I will draw on a radical yet silenced narrative of recent church history in Britain that sought to educate for class consciousness in the context of Christian formation: the Socialist Sunday School movement. In doing so, I will argue that there is a need to 'storm the heavens' of theological education institutes and bring about solidarity among working-class clergy, ordinands and educators, as a means of organizing in the struggle not just for working-class representation in church ministry, but also for class consciousness and social transformation within and outside of the Church.

Class in the classroom in theological education in the UK

Theological education has the ability to reinforce notions of class hierarchy and enable cultures of deference to the middle and upper classes; this is often influenced by the culture of the institutions as well as the pedagogy and curricula. Take, for example, the words of one student who was training for ministry in the Church of England at a theological education institute in the UK:

> I am a working-class woman who has given up so much to be here and follow my calling to serve Jesus, but I constantly feel like I don't fit in. I can't relate to the books I read, I feel uncomfortable speaking out when I don't agree, I don't want to say when I can't make it to something because I have to look after my family member – because this just makes me look weak, and every doubt that the BAP had in me will be shown to be true.[11]

Theological Education Institutes (TEIs) in the UK were not made to accommodate the experiences of working-class women and men. Students often struggle to reconcile their working-class background and lived experiences with the middle-class environments of the TEIs, and this is further impacted by the fact that the majority of educators are middle class. The student's narrative speaks to what Bourdieu has referred to as 'habitus', where the student enters an environment where they feel as though they do not belong and are destabilized in the process.[12] This can lead to working-class students feeling a sense of shame and social isolation, and in the context of spiritual formation, a sense of spiritual shame, where they feel as though they are somehow neglecting or failing their 'calling'. The sense of habitus dislocation creates a feeling of unworthiness; this is outlined by the words of another student, who stated:

> I have been called lazy because I wasn't able to make a deadline, they didn't believe me that I had finished a late shift at work, had to look after my mum and the kids and it was impossible to make the deadline they expected. I ended up having to have a meeting with someone high up the chain who explained to me that if I lied to get out of submitting work that was on me and my conscience. They even said to me that I had deliberately plagiarized. I didn't but they didn't believe me so I failed that assignment.[13]

This student outlines how they have been stereotyped as 'lazy' and in many ways made to feel like an outsider in the context of the higher education institute. The notion of 'shift work' is clearly not understood by those with the power in the TEI and this relates to the habitus of the middle class, where certain lived experiences are taken for granted, such as not needing to work alongside studying. To refer to another of Bourdieu's central concepts, the notion of the 'field' of education is also relevant here:

> The field is a social space where people perform daily actions. It is structured by rules that shape habitus ... the common characteristic of all fields is that they are arenas of struggle where social actors strategise, manoeuvre and vie for recognition.[14]

The student struggles in a field of theological education that has been geared against them, because caring responsibilities and the need for paid employment are not the norm. This comes to the detriment of the student's studies and their experience of higher education, where they are fundamentally made to feel they do not belong. As Richard Jenkins has remarked, each field 'is both the product and producer of the habitus which is specific and appropriate to the field'.[15] The field of theological education has been determined by the habitus of the middle and upper classes and this is also made apparent in the dominant pedagogies and curricula. Curricula in theological education are often dominated by white male middle-class theologians, who determine what does and not qualify as real knowledge. Class inequality therefore often remains a silenced reality and the curriculum serves to reinforce the middle-class habitus. This is an issue of unequal distribution of knowledge, particularly when we consider knowledge as capital. What becomes apparent as we look at reading lists and staff representation, for example, is that the epistemology of the middle class is privileged over and against that of the working class, who are predominantly ignored. This is also apparent in dominant pedagogies that foster a middle-class habitus where the lived experiences and emotions of students are often not respected as worthy knowledge to be shared in the classroom. One student highlighted this in describing her experience of being 'humiliated and embarrassed' by having been silenced for sharing in the classroom her embodied narrative of abuse.[16] Pedagogies and curricula that deny the embodied experiences and struggles of students only serve to reinforce the hierarchies of oppression that have pushed certain groups of people to the margins. Theological education that operates under the middle-class habitus operates to justify class hierarchy because students are expected to conform to certain middle-class norms.

Class also continues to have significant implications for those who complete their academic formation for ordination, for example, but then struggle to get 'jobs'. Diane Reay makes a similar point in her recent study of working-class progression in higher education, noting that:

> The commonplace assumption is that getting more working-class young people going to university is an unmitigated success. Yet behind that rosy view are hidden troubling issues around whether a working-class student's degree has the same value as a middle- or upper-class student's degree.[17]

Further, working-class students are often forced into certain roles within church ministry as a result of their class status, as one student remarked:

> I had a tutor who told me I could only serve on estates because of the way I spoke and how I dressed. He said I was exactly what the church needed though in reaching out to the 'unchurched' and 'illiterate'. He said the working class, like me, need God urgently because there are so many single mums, hoodies, and drugs that they need salvation and they need it fast.[18]

The reality is that working-class students are also often not being given the adequate support to prepare for the realities of class inequality, where 'working-class graduates ... are the most likely to end up in working-class jobs'.[19] What becomes apparent then, in the case of the Church of England in particular, is that while there have been certain commitments to address the 'barriers' to the working class being accepted into formational training for ministry,[20] 'little has been done to address the class disparities and the implications of class struggle in theological education and formation.'[21] The field of theological education in the UK seemingly serves to validate class hierarchy and social norms that operate to the detriment of the working class. The students' narratives support this argument, noting that working-class students often struggle to recognize themselves as 'worthy' of being in formational training. However, the response to such inequality must not be for the working class to remove themselves from the academic institutions of power, or to succumb to the notion that education belongs to the middle class, but instead, in agreement with Bourdieu, to recognize that:

> The intellectual world must engage in a permanent critique of all the abuses of power or authority committed in the name of intellectual authority, or, if you prefer, in a relentless critique of the use of intellectual authority as a political weapon within the intellectual field.[22]

The struggle is then to engage and subvert the structures of TEIs, to educate for liberation and class consciousness. By doing this, students of theology might not only interpret the world in a theological sense, but intervene, change and challenge it.

Learning from the Socialist Sunday Schools

In 1892 Mary Gray was running a soup kitchen for the children of the dock strikers in London. She became aware of what little education the children had received and the impact this was having on the raging inequality within Britain. That year she founded the Socialist Sunday School in Battersea, London, which intentionally taught socialist ideals and morals to children. Three years later a movement of such Sunday schools had been set up in working-class areas of Britain, including in Glasgow, Edinburgh, Yorkshire, Lancashire and London. As Thomas Linehan remarks:

> By 1907, London boasted over 20 Socialist Sunday Schools. By 1912 there were around 96 schools spread around the country, catering for an estimated 4540 children ... the Socialist Sunday Schools sought to nurture the child's natural moral sensibilities by encouraging the ethic of social sympathy and co-operative solidarity.[23]

In many of the schools those enrolled were predominantly working-class girls and young women.[24] The Socialist Sunday School movement was birthed in response to 'social inequalities and the deficiencies of state schooling'. Jessica Gerrard comments that they aimed 'to create alternative educational experiences for children and young people, and attempted to challenge the classed positions'.[25] The pedagogy of the schools was strongly influenced by dominant church Sunday schools, as teaching often involved hymns, activities and the learning of the ten socialist commandments that became known as precepts, and professed a need for social justice and class consciousness. The schools taught:

That morality is the fulfilment of one's duty to one's neighbour ... That the present social system is devoid of the elements of love or justice, since, as an organisation, it ignores
the claims of the weak and distressed, and that is, therefore
immoral.[26]

Though they did not require those who attended to be Christian,
the schools were often rooted in Christian socialist ideals. Alongside academic reading and writing, the schools taught solidarity
and compassion as a means of challenging dominant ideologies
and pedagogies that silenced the working-class experience. The
educators also gave focus to class social interdependence and
cooperative social and industrial action.[27]

The Socialist Sunday Schools offer an example of a concrete
alternative that contemporary theological education institutes
can learn from for the sake of critical pedagogy in the process
of formation. This is particularly relevant given the time in
which formation for ministry is currently taking place, because
I write during the so-called winter of discontent, where nurses
are on strike for the first time in the history of the NHS and
churches are being used as 'warm banks' to offer a safe and
warm space for people during a cost-of-living crisis. Food-bank
usage is at an all-time high, and lack of adequate funding to
state schools across Britain is impacting working-class children
the hardest.[28] These social realities matter greatly to those in
formational ministry because the needs of the working class
in Britain are fundamental to the purpose and survival of the
Church. Theological education that aims to educate those
about the world 'that faith creates and inhabits'[29] must then
ask critical questions about the purpose and role of ministry
in the context of Britain today, where 'warm banks' and 'food
banks' are shaping much of church ministry. There is also a
need to reflect critically on the dominant knowledge structures
that are in place in theological education: as church buildings
become warm banks and food banks, is there not a need to educate those in formation for ministry about the contemporary
socio-economic relations that have brought about the need for
so-called 'charity'? Once we start to raise such questions, they

lead us to thinking about who is in charge of what we learn and how we learn in theological education. How do the reading lists for those in ministerial formation support those seeking to address the systemic realities of poverty and inequality? Will formational education teach those in ministry to accept such inequalities or will it teach them to challenge such injustices, and if so, how? How do existing pedagogies engage with the fact that many of those in training for ministry are also reliant on such charity to survive?[30]

It is here that we could learn from the curricula of the Socialist Sunday Schools (SSS). They were often radical because they aimed to challenge the dominant and 'indoctrinating' state education system that was shaped to instil deference to the status quo that favoured the wealthy elites. The SSS curriculum aimed to create a counterbalance: 'they taught science, literature, socialist interpretations of history and cooperative ethics, and involved students in a range of activities to encourage cooperative and socialist outlook and culture, from needlecraft to rambling, participation in May Day marches, and singing.'[31] The children of the Socialist Sunday Schools also became educators in their own right: their writing in *The Young Socialist* magazine included poems for children, lesson ideas, reports and social campaigns. The aim of the educator was to encourage critical thinking alongside class consciousness, as Kendrick Shedd noted when speaking to the teachers of the Socialist Sunday Schools in the USA:

> Let us set the children thinking. Let us encourage intelligent questions. We want the little ones to grow up with inquiring minds. Can you help them to do this? Let us try to help them to get the economic viewpoint, the viewpoint of the working class.[32]

Education was shaped around the need to think critically and justly, and to take into consideration the social context in which those in the learning institutes were engaged and lived. As Kenneth Teitelbaum comments:

Unlike the traditional topics that are found in public school textbooks, with rather idealized middle-class versions of family and community life, these materials include lessons on such themes as 'Unemployment, Poverty and Drink', 'Slums, Sweatshops, Sickness and Disease,' and 'Why Johnny Loses His Home' ... the primary focus was on the economic pressures that make working-class life so difficult.[33]

The schools responded to societal needs and so were contextually relevant; curricula were focused on the collective and aimed to challenge hegemonic knowledge systems, socioeconomic relations and unjust ideologies: 'As such, the Socialist Sunday schools' curriculum carried the potential for human liberation in that it sought to advance epistemologies that resisted the status quo relations and enable students to develop forms of consciousness that fostered collective action against mass exploitation.'[34] While the Socialist Sunday Schools represent a model of subversive education, they did not escape certain hegemonic norms such as gender, which as Jessica Gerrard remarks, 'haunted the movement's broader function and representation ... much SSS curriculum implicitly and explicitly supported gendered divisions of labour by drawing heavily on socialist articulations of the family as a symbol of a natural state of cooperative politics.'[35] The focus of children's education also differs from theological education and the formation of adults for ministry; indeed, the purpose of the SSS was not to teach Christianity. However, my aim in sharing a piece of working-class history that has been written out of hegemonic British history is to outline what is possible when the working class organize to educate for social transformation and class consciousness, and to capture the ways in which progressive and critical pedagogy can 'challenge the presumption of working-class incapability'.[36] In this model of teaching, trust is placed in the lived experiences of the working class, as one student commented:

What pleases us most, I think, is the trust the teachers put in us, we really and actually carry on the schools ourselves with the exception of the teaching and even there we are encouraged to express exactly what we think.[37]

This differs greatly from the experiences described by the working-class students in theological education institutes in the UK. The Socialist Sunday School movement was eventually brought to an end as a result of conservative action to shut down the schools by banning them from operating in council buildings and coordinating a parliamentary hearing of the Seditious Teaching Bill, which sought to ban socialist teachings. In the words of Paulo Freire, 'it would indeed be naïve to expect the oppressor elites to carry out a liberating education.'[38] This was an education born out of the collective struggles of the working class, the demand for change and the awareness that systemic transformation is not possible without working-class education. Education is not therefore something to be deemed elitist and reserved to privilege the middle and upper class; it is a critical tool to be used by the collective to challenge the injustices of working-class conditions, because without organized educated resistance, solidarity will not be achieved and social transformation will not happen.

Educating for class consciousness

When we enter the classroom, we each come with our own stories. Educators, as well as students, carry narratives, experiences and struggles. As a theological educator I have pushed what Robin DiAngelo refers to as the twin 'boulders' of classism and sexism, and while this has no doubt led to a lack of self-confidence, a sense of imposter syndrome, and many anecdotal examples of being patronized and mocked, I am also aware that like DiAngelo, my 'white privilege' has helped me to manage class and gender inequalities,[39] noting that: 'Black academics, especially BME women from working-class backgrounds, face triple oppression – gender, ethnicity and class.'[40] Theological education remains a field of middle-class dispositions, and this became extremely apparent when I was researching the barriers to belonging for those in formational training for ministry in the UK, where working-class students persistently described feelings of unbelonging, marginalization and explicit class discrimination. The curriculum in theological education institutes often reinforces the culture, history, perspectives and epistemology of the white, male, middle and upper class, thereby reinforcing the middle-class status quo, where critical and transformative pedagogy is deemed inappropriate in the face of tradition. What also became apparent in researching barriers to belonging in theological education is that the educator who seeks to educate for class consciousness must be counter-cultural because the present curricula and dominant pedagogies are shaped by the norms of the liberal elites and the culturally conservative. This is made apparent by the ways in which theological education is often separated from the life and struggles of the students, which has pedagogical consequences, as Bernhard Ott has noted, because: 'If we assume that in a course of training and study certain skills are to be learned, the gap between the context of study and the context of life proves fatal.'[41] As a result, working-class epistemology has been marginalized from dominant ways of knowing and contemplating God and Christian praxis.

Curriculum in theological education continues to be a much-debated subject. Edward Farley, for example, suggests that: 'theological education is no longer the reflection of faith that leads to the understanding of God but rather has become nothing more than an intellectual exercise in fulfilling an academic curriculum. And thereby the heart of theological education has been lost.'[42] However, theology as an intellectual exercise is of significant importance in the process of formation, particularly if it is relevant to the lived experiences of the students. The intellectual exercise of thinking critically enables contemplation of God and the Christian faith in a way that helps students to reflect and engage with the world that faith inhabits, the society that church is lived in, and the context in which the student is learning to decode. If the curriculum supports such intellectual contemplation and reflective theology, it has the potential to be liberative and transformative. The difficulty arises when the knowledge that shapes the curricula is determined solely by the privileged elites and is removed from the day-to-day struggles of the marginalized. A curriculum that offers the space for theological contemplation that is rooted in such struggles would enable a model of learning that is shaped by reflection and action in the world. According to Ivan Illich:

> A good educational system should have three purposes: it should provide all who want to learn with access to available resources at any time in their lives; empower all who want to share what they know to find those who want to learn it from them; and, finally, furnish all who want to present an issue to the public with the opportunity to make their challenge known.[43]

The difficulty at present for many working-class students in theological education is that they do not feel 'empowered to share' in the classroom, the resources are often unrelatable to the working-class experience, and the dominant pedagogies often do not encourage critical thinking that arises out of lived working-class experiences. Yet the hope is that the words of bell hooks ring true, that:

> The classroom with all its limitations remains a location of possibility. In that field of possibility, we have the opportunity to labour for freedom, to demand of ourselves and our comrades an openness of mind and heart that allows us to face reality even as we collectively imagine ways to move beyond boundaries, to transgress. This is education for the practice of freedom.[44]

If theological education is to educate for the 'practice of freedom' and enable students to contemplate God in ways that can prevent working-class students from feeling marginalized, isolated and without agency, it will teach to empower and to journey with God through the daily struggles in ways that are liberative. Such an education is not centred on naïve notions of superficial Christian joy that are ignorant of the struggles of the oppressed and the truth of the suffering of Christ on the cross, because educating for class consciousness demands that the educator does not succumb to a passive pedagogy that is ignorant of class injustice. It is best summarized by hooks, who writes:

> To educate as the practice of freedom is a way of teaching that anyone can learn. That learning process comes easiest to those of us who teach who also believe that there is an aspect of our vocation that is sacred; who believe that our work is not merely to share information but to share in the intellectual and spiritual growth of our students. To teach in a manner that respects and cares for the souls of our students is essential if we are to provide the necessary conditions where learning can most deeply and intimately begin.[45]

This is what it means to teach to transgress the boundaries of class while joining students in the struggle. Intellectual growth and spiritual growth are not separate but intertwined; therefore, when working-class students enter the classroom for formation in theological education, education can become the armour by which the working class learns to resist the class bias of the Church and society. In doing so, the working-class student can become the agent of social, political and theological change.

Conclusion

Working-class clergy, laypeople, ordinands, ministers in training and theological educators can learn from British working-class history what it means to collectively organize and educate for change. Solidarity is critical, because those who maintain the power will seek to silence and oppress those who work in ways that aim to challenge the status quo. The experiences of working-class students, which I have outlined in this chapter, are not isolated incidents of marginalization and class-based oppression but are shared by many of the working class both within and outside theological education. Therefore, if theological education is to be transformed in a way that encourages social transformation, it must enable class consciousness through critical pedagogy and a transformed curriculum that offers the space for voices that encourage radical Christian theologies of liberation for the oppressed. Just as the Socialist Sunday Schools came about as organized acts of resistance against the injustices of capitalist greed, today theological education must become conscious of what it means to educate for formation during a cost-of-living crisis that is pushing millions more people into poverty, in a context of soaring levels of wealth inequality, child poverty, austerity and in a nation where the privileged political elites are choosing to bring about the collapse of the National Health Service and failing to adequately support schools, councils and basic services. There is no choice for the working class but to educate, agitate and organize.

Notes

1 H. Quelch, 1902, quoted in Karl Kautsky, 'Clericalism and the Socialist Attitude Thereto: A Symposium', *Social Democrat*, 7, 4 (April 1903).

2 Jonathan Rose, 2021, *The Intellectual Life of the British Working Classes*, Third edition, New Haven, CT and London: Yale University Press, p. 23.

3 See Madeleine Davies, 2018, 'Selection procedures "favour middle class"' in *Church Times*, 27 April, https://www.churchtimes.co.uk/articles/2018/27-april/news/uk/selection-procedures-favour-middle-class (accessed 22.03.2023).

4 See Elliot B. Weininger, 'Foundations of Pierre Bourdieu's Class Analysis', in *Approaches to Class Analysis*, ed. Erik Olin Wright (Cambridge: Cambridge University Press, 2005), p. 86.

5 Pierre Bourdieu, 1984, *Distinction: A Social Critique of the Judgement of Taste*, Richard Nice (trans.), Cambridge, MA: Harvard University Press, p. 114.

6 Katie Beswick, 'Feeling Working Class: Affective Class Identification and its Implications for Overcoming Inequality', *Studies in Theatre and Performance*, 40, 3 (2020), pp. 265–74; pp. 265–6.

7 The British Election Study found that those who identify as working class in Britain have remained in the majority: 'Even though the proportion of people doing a working class job has declined, the level of identification with the working class has proven to be a remarkably stable feature of British society.' See Geoffrey Evans and Jonathan

Mellon, 'Social Class: Identity, Awareness and Political Attitudes: Why are We Still Working Class?' *British Social Attitudes*, 33 (2016) online, https://www.bsa.natcen.ac.uk/media/39094/bsa33_social-class_v5.pdf (accessed 22.03.2023).

8 See Joshua Taylor, 2019, 'Boris Johnson called Working Class Men "drunk, criminal and feckless"', *The Mirror*, 28 November, available online: https://www.mirror.co.uk/news/politics/boris-johnson-called-working-class-20981604 (accessed 22.03.2023).

9 The leader of the Labour Party has repeatedly refused to support industrial disputes, despite workers across the country, including nurses, lecturers, train drivers and postal workers, calling for solidarity with the strikes. See Matthew Weaver, 2022, 'Keir Starmer Repeatedly Refuses to Back Striking Workers', *The Guardian*, 6 October, available online, https://www.theguardian.com/politics/2022/oct/06/keir-starmer-repeat edly-refuses-to-back-striking-workers (accessed 22.03.2023).

10 Rowan Williams quoted by Benjamin Wayman, 2020, 'Rowan Williams: Theological Education Is for Everyone', *Christianity Today*, 19 August, available online: https://www.christianitytoday.com/ct/2020/august-web-only/rowan-williams-theological-education-for-everyone.html (accessed 22.03.2023).

11 BAP refers to the Bishop's Advisory Panel of the Church of England, a process that is undertaken by those who feel 'called' into ministry. The student's comments are based on research undertaken by the author in 2019–2021 with the Common Awards team at the University of Durham. See Eve Parker, 2022, *Trust in Theological Education: Deconstructing 'Trustworthiness' for a Pedagogy of Liberation*, London: SCM Press, p. 89.

12 See Terry Eagleton and Pierre Bourdieu, 'Doxa and Common Life', *New Left Review*, 1, 191 (1992), p. 117.

13 See Parker, *Trust in Theological Education*, p. 65.

14 See Stan Houston and Calvin Swords, 'Responding to the "Weight of the World": Unveiling the "Feeling" Bourdieu in Social Work', *The British Journal of Social Work*, 55, 4 (2022), pp. 1934–51.

15 R. Jenkins, 2007, *Pierre Bourdieu*, London: Routledge, p. 84.

16 See Parker, *Trust in Theological Education*, p. 43.

17 Diane Reay, 'The Working Classes and Higher Education: Merito-cratic Fallacies of Upward Mobility in the United Kingdom', *European Journal of Education*, 56, 1 (2021), pp. 53–64; p. 54.

18 See Parker, *Trust in Theological Education*, p. 63.

19 Reay, 'The Working Classes and Higher Education', p. 54.

20 See Madeleine Davies, 2021, 'Is the CofE still a Class-Riddled Act?', *Church Times*, 25 June, https://www.churchtimes.co.uk/articles/2021/25-june/features/features/is-the-c-of-e-still-a-class-riddled-act (accessed 22.03.2023).

21 See Parker, *Trust in Theological Education*, p. 64.

22 Pierre Bourdieu, 'For a Scholarship with Commitment', *Profession* (2000), pp. 40–45, 41.

23 Thomas Linehan, 2012, *Modernism and British Socialism*, New York: Palgrave Macmillan, p. 114.

24 N. C. Rafeek, 'Against the Odds: Women in the Communist Party in Scotland 1920–91: An Oral History', PhD thesis, 1998. University of Strathclyde.

25 Jessica Gerrard, 2014, *Radical Childhoods*, New York: Manchester University Press.

26 Working Class Movement Library, 'Socialist Sunday Schools', *Working Class Movement Library*, https://www.wcml.org.uk/our-collections/creativity-and-culture/leisure/socialist-sunday-schools/ (accessed 22.03.2023).

27 This is made apparent in the last two precepts: 'Do not think that he who loves his own country must hate and despise other nations, or wish for war, which is a remnant of barbarism. Look forward to the day when all men will be free citizens of one fatherland and live together as brothers in peace and righteousness.' Quoted by Cyril Pearce, 2001, *Comrades in Conscience: The Story of an English Community's Opposition to the Great War*, London: Francis Boutle Publishers, p. 53.

28 In 2022 over 68% of primary schools in the UK reported getting insufficient funding from the government to support pupils. See Bethan Staton, 'UK Schools warn Lack of "Catch-Up" Funding is Hitting Lost Learning', *Financial Times*, https://www.ft.com/content/2fd514db-2a73-4c76-bb67-7fbf067ced74 (accessed 22.03.2023).

29 Williams quoted by Wayman, 'Rowan Williams: Theological Education Is for Everyone'.

30 In the spring of 2022, the Church of England announced that it will have to increase the amount of funding for hardship grants to support clergy and lay workers struggling with the cost-of-living crisis. See Church of England, 2022, 'Up to £3 Million to boost Diocesan Discretionary Funds in Face of Rising Cost of Living', *The Church of England*, 9 May, https://www.churchofengland.org/media-and-news/press-releases/ps3-million-boost-diocesan-discretionary-funds-face-rising-cost (accessed 22.03.2023).

31 Gerrard, *Radical Childhoods*.

32 Quoted by Kenneth Teitelbaum, 'Critical Lesson from Our Past: Curricula of Socialist Sunday Schools in the United States', *Curriculum Inquiry*, 20, 4 (1990), pp. 407–436; p. 421.

33 Teitelbaum, 'Critical Lesson from Our Past', p. 423.

34 Wayne Au, 2012, *Critical Curriculum Studies: Education, Consciousness, and the Politics of Knowing*, New York: Routledge, p. 73.

35 Jessica Gerrard, '"Little Soldiers" for Socialism: Childhood and Socialist Politics in the British Socialist Sunday School Movement', *International Review of Social History*, 58, 1 (2013), pp. 71–96; p. 90.

36 Gerrard, '"Little Soldiers" for Socialism', p. 91.

37 Gerrard, '"Little Soldiers" for Socialism', p. 92.

38 Paulo Freire, 2005, *Pedagogy of the Oppressed*, New York: Continuum, p. 134.

39 See Robin DiAngelo, 2012, *What Does it Mean to Be White? Developing White Racial Literacy*, New York: Peter Lang.

40 Teresa Crew, 2020, *Higher Education and Working-Class Academics: Precarity and Diversity in Academia*, Basingstoke: Palgrave Pivot, p. 4.

41 Bernhard Ott, 2016, *Understanding and Developing Theological Education*, Cumbria: Langham Partnership, p. 44.

42 See Ott, *Understanding and Developing Theological Education*, p. 40.

43 Ivan Illich, 1971, *Deschooling Society*, London: Calder & Boyars, p. 75.

44 bell hooks, 1989, *Talking Back: Thinking Feminist, Thinking Black*, Boston, MA: South End Press, p. 207.

45 bell hooks, 1994 *Teaching to Transgress: Education as the Practice of Freedom*, New York: Routledge, p. 13.

9

Conclusion:
The Spirit and Struggling
for Solidarity

FR LUKE LARNER

The most important word in the language of the working class is 'solidarity'.[1]

The claims of the gospel are ones that call for radical solidarity, one with another, across lines of ethnic, gender and class distinctions.[2]

Over the last three years the word 'solidarity' has become increasingly important to me. It all started in the unlikely environment of the Common Room at Ripon College Cuddesdon, where Fr Rajiv (author of Chapter 3) and I trained for ordination in the Church of England. It's fair to say that this quaint Neo-gothic Anglican college in the Oxfordshire countryside (or 'Holy Hogwarts' as we called it) isn't known as a hotbed of radical class discourse! But it was there that I started to see the theme of solidarity as an important next step in working out how to weave together my working-class background, my experiences as a lay minister in the post-industrial town of Luton, my soon-to-be vocation as a priest, and my theological work. I owe a debt of gratitude to Fr Rajiv and my dissertation tutor, Revd Dr Susie Snyder, for the conversations (often in the common room bar) that pointed me in the direction of solidarity as a key theme. Soon after these conversations took place,

I was deployed 20 miles north from Luton to Bedford's town centre (which felt quite posh in comparison) to serve as a curate in the Civic and Country Church of St Paul.

Just outside Bedford town is the notorious Yarl's Wood Immigration Removal Centre, where people are detained before being deported out of the UK. At this time the UK government was ramping up its 'hostile environment' strategy towards refugees and asylum seekers, a phenomenon that has continued for the last two years under two Home Secretaries known for their cruel and dehumanizing rhetoric. Soon after arriving in Bedford, I became aware of a plan to house a large number of people seeking asylum in portacabins adjacent to the security perimeter of Yarl's Wood IRC. This was in the height of the second wave of Covid when people staying in other notorious sites (such as Napier Barracks) were experiencing big Covid outbreaks and suffering terribly. Joining with a friend from the Council of Mosques in Luton and a variety of local activists, we resisted these cruel and dehumanizing plans (and we won). The slogan of an organization that I turned to for help and advice (and have done many times since) is 'Solidarity Knows No Borders'.[3] In later actions that year, not least protesting planned deportation flights to Rwanda, we chanted and sang those words, often to the accompaniment of a raucous samba band. I remember standing with a large and diverse crowd of activists (including a couple of other 'lefty priests' in cassocks) and singing in call-and-response across the detention centre fence with those poor souls facing forced displacement. It was one of the most profound experiences of my life.

In the summer of 2022, I joined a few friends (including Vic Turner, author of Chapter 7 and Joerg Rieger, who generously wrote our Afterword) for our inaugural panel on Class and Religion at the European Academy of Religion in the Italian city of Bologna (which, unlike Cuddesdon, really is a hotbed of class discourse!). One of the topics that came up in our panel (I think prompted by Prof. Mario Aguilar) was the ongoing strike action back in the UK, not least the firebrand leadership of RMT leader Mick Lynch. Professor Aguilar offered the challenge that church in the UK should be offering outspoken support for organized labour fighting for better pay and conditions. Predictably, some voices in the Church have responded to the RMT strikes with the typical 'we agree with your goals but not your means of getting there' rhetoric. As a union member myself (yes, even clergy can unionize!), I wondered what it meant in theology and praxis to show solidarity with the workers, especially as the words 'cost-of-living crisis' loomed in the air.

In the middle of these turbulent years, the former Archbishop of Canterbury, Rowan Williams, gave the 2021 Ken Leech memorial lecture on the theme of solidarity, which spoke profoundly to the ideas I was wrestling with. Williams, drawing from Leech, described solidarity as 'recognising shared interest and undertaking shared risk'.[4] Through expressing solidarity in theological language, Williams suggested that it is not an *ideal* or another ethical or religious 'ought to', but rather 'it is something that exists in the very charter of our humanity.' For Williams, solidarity is part of what it means to be human, it is to protest 'against those forces that challenge and oppose a mutuality already given by God' in recognition that human beings in virtue of our very creation are bound to one another in solidarity.[5] In the post-Covid, cost-of-living crisis, hostile environment world we inhabit as we write this book, it is important, I believe, to recognize this idea of solidarity as both inherently human and as God-given. Solidarity is not something we can simply drum up. Indeed, a poignant reminder of this was the 'clap for our care workers' phenomenon during the Covid lockdowns of 2020, whereby the then prime minister Boris Johnson encouraged people to stand on their doorstep banging pots and pans in supposed solidarity with front-line health-care staff. Despite this huge outpouring of public and government support, UK nurses and other medical practitioners are having to join many other workers in taking nationwide strike action for better pay and conditions. Multi-millionaire Prime Minister Rishi Sunak has said that the asks of the nurses and other key workers are simply unaffordable, despite the billions doled out in dodgy contracts for PPE and other Covid-related scandals over the last few years. As Rowan Williams observes in a more recent article on the cost-of-living crisis, it is disappointing that while we recognized 'that no one is safe unless everyone is safe' during the pandemic, many seem to have failed to recognize 'that this applies to our economic as much as our medical wellbeing' for as long as we tolerate 'a social order where precariousness is so unevenly shared'.[6]

In this concluding chapter, I will draw together the threads of what we have discussed so far as a diverse group of Christian working-class theologians, by exploring the theme of solidarity in conversation with Christian understandings of the Holy Spirit (known as pneumatology in academic theology). I'm indebted to the inspirational work of my friends and co-authors in this book for so excellently exploring: (1) Intersectional experiences of class and the Church, (2) Class leadership in mission and ministry, and (3) Class, solidarity and the struggle for the common good. I will structure my closing reflections on these three themes in the following way:

1 Experiences: Theosis and mass movements
2 Leadership: The Spirit and the voice of the prophets
3 Solidarity and the struggle for the common good: Organizing as a *missio Spiritus*

Theosis and mass movements

In the opening chapter of this book, I critiqued theological approaches to class that I described as 'feckless faith'. These offer a shallow approach to class that is often immaterial and individualistic in the hope it offers, focusing on working-class church membership and (at best) working-class church leadership. 'Feckless faith' fails to critique labour relationships and economic injustice, it fails to draw on the myriad voices engaging with these questions from other disciplines and perspectives. The experiences shared in the first chapters of this book, from three very different perspectives and sets of experiences, demonstrate how big an issue this is. In our proposal for our second panel on class at the European Academy of Religion in 2023, Victoria Turner (author of Chapter 7) described how we are seeking to 'extend the notion of class beyond surface level ideas of cultural capital, sociological belonging, and scapegoating rhetoric' and look to 'explore class from a perspective of economic exploitation and the shared struggle of the majority to live in a system of competition, deceit and marginalisation'. By trying to engage with class and associated issues like economic exploitation and marginalization under capitalism, we are wanting to do deeper theological reflection on these issues, asking how they relate to our understanding of God, our understanding of mission and our understanding of what church is and is for.

My own academic research has a particular focus on the Holy Spirit, and I believe that engaging these class issues through theologies of the Holy Spirit offers some new perspectives. This may all seem quite lofty language for a book addressing the struggles of the working classes; indeed, I have been criticized for 'pretending to be working class' by clerical colleagues who think it impossible that a working-class person could be well read and engage in academic discourse in an outspoken fashion. This anti-intellectualism, as Eve Parker observes in her chapter, is another example of a surface-level feckless-faith approach to class and hinders Christian engagement in class struggle. By drawing from theologies of the Holy Spirit I want to argue that some of the central pillars of my faith and my practice, both as a baptized Christian and as a priest in God's Church, specifically relate to theologies of class.

Having been formed for the priesthood in the more catholic end of the Church of England, the celebration of the Eucharist (also known as 'The Mass', 'communion' or 'The Lord's Supper') has become central to my faith, spirituality and practice. I believe that the Eucharist is more than a memorial meal or ritual but is rather a *sacrament*. Saint Augustine was the first to describe sacraments as 'an outward and visible sign of an inward and invisible grace'. Sacraments are more than an act, they are something visible and physical through which God brings transformation. Fr Rajiv described in Chapter 3 how some of the words we Anglicans use in our eucharistic celebration impact on his understanding of class and solidarity: 'Jesus humbled himself to share in our humanity.' Our common humanity, as Rowan Williams described, exists within the given-ness of our humanity, and God not only gives us this, but *enters into this solidarity* in Jesus' incarnation as a human being. This is part of what we are celebrating, and I believe entering into ourselves, when we share that Eucharist feast. Tim Gorringe recognizes this understanding of the Eucharist in the work of the radical Anglo-Catholic priest Alan Ecclestone:

> The Eucharist speaks of commitment to God's Kingdom ('sacrifice'), the sanctity of material things, and the new community. When the whole human race is living the life symbolised in the Mass, living in comradeship and equality, sharing all the material things of the world and all the joys of life in common, then the whole world will be seen to be the very body and blood of God. Thus the Mass is both the foretaste of the Divine Commonwealth, which is the true natural human life, and a means for bringing it about.[7]

This understanding draws from the legacy of radical Anglo-Catholic social teaching – a legacy that some of the authors of this book seek to continue. A common practice in Anglo-Catholic churches is to reserve some of the consecrated bread after communion, which is then often distributed to the sick and housebound. Gorringe goes on to highlight the depth of belief that some radical Anglo-Catholics had in this solidarity by sharing the words of a sign often placed by the reserved sacrament, which warned:

> Unless you see Christ in the masses you cannot see Him in the Mass. Unless you see Him in Communism you will not see Him in Communion. Unless you see Him in the workers' struggle for bread you will not see Him at the altar. Unless you are revolutionary against the present evil world, which denies the bread of life to those who produce it, and unless you fight for the common bread for the common people you must not dare to approach this holy sacrament.[8]

The implications of these words are clear – to deny divine investment in class struggle is to fail to understand the nature of communion. More specifically, a failure to discern the work of God in class struggle is a *denial of the transformative work of the Spirit*. One of the high points in the celebration of the Eucharist in many traditions is the invocation of the Holy Spirit over the elements of bread and wine. This is called the *epiclesis*. The Eastern Orthodox tradition emphasizes the *epiclesis* as the key moment where Christ becomes somehow mysteriously present in the Eucharist; the invoking of the Spirit brings the transformation. The Russian Orthodox theologian Sergei Bulgakov saw profound implications for this understanding of the Spirit's work of transformation. Drawing from the traditional Orthodox teaching of *theosis*, he saw that the Spirit's transforming work in the Eucharist is continued as the Spirit is invoked upon God's people to transform them, raising them through Christ into the life of God just as the bread and wine are raised during the consecration. Bulgakov saw the continued work of the Spirit post-Pentecost as 'invisibly transfiguring' the world, and indeed the human race – for 'The Holy Spirit inspires humanity, thereby taking part in its history.'[9] When we consider the implications of these understandings of the work of the Spirit, when we recognize that the Spirit raises human society into the kind of communion (*koinonia*) represented by the Lord's Supper, when we acknowledge that that same Spirit enflamed the hearts of the prophets who raged against the oppression of the poor, it is my belief that we can come to a simple conclusion: The mission of the Spirit of God, in part at least, *is the empowerment of class struggle and eradication of unjust class structures*. This, for me, has profoundly changed and shaped my understanding and experience of partaking in and celebrating the Lord's supper whereby the Spirit is invoked on the rudimentary things of life – bread and wine – in the hope of transformation.

It can sometimes be helpful to demonstrate a point by considering its opposite. If we are to believe that, as Bulgakov contends, the Spirit is at work in the transfiguring of human beings and the world – do we really believe that this transformation will maintain existing class structures that depend on the exploitation of workers (and indeed the planet itself)? Is the work of the Spirit to enable the continued wage theft of the labouring majority in favour of the wealthy few? Is the work of the Spirit to continue abjectly undemocratic labour relations that leave the means of production in the hands of the few? No – it cannot be, for this is the antithesis of that which we celebrate when we gather around the Lord's table. It is, in fact, a blasphemy. For 'where the Spirit of the Lord is, there is *freedom*' (2 Corinthians 3.17 NRSV).

In our present moment, then, we might consider those class movements that lead us towards a global sense of *koinonia* to be *Mass movements* (in the eucharistic sense) because at their best they too could be considered a sign and foretaste of where the Spirit is leading us, and a means of getting us there. This broader emphasis on mass movements does not of course ignore the personal transformation that needs to occur in the individuals who participate in movements. To paraphrase a recent speech by Cornel West, it is only through this spiritual transformation that I am able to find love for my wicked neighbour in my own wicked heart. We must, however, reject an individualist concept of the Spirit's work that focuses on personal piety alone. I'm drawn at this point to Ruth Harley's use of the wilderness metaphor in her chapter. As painful as time in the wilderness can be, it is characteristic of the Spirit to lead God's people through the wilderness. The Spirit led Jesus to the wilderness after his baptism to test his resistance to the temptation of grasping worldly power and wealth, just as the Spirit led God's people to liberation through the wilderness in the Exodus narrative. The journey is long and hard and can leave us longing for the fleshpots of Egypt, but it is through Exodus that we are delivered by the Spirit into liberation and the emancipation that comes through Jubilee. Let us not forget, of course, that the Exodus narrative occurs specifically in the context of labour exploitation and leads to justice and the redistribution of land and access to the means of production in the promised land. The liberation theologian Jorge Pixley recognizes in his commentary on Exodus that this message resonates with mass movements today, 'wherever the text of Exodus is read by anyone sensitive to what God wants to do today in the liberation of oppressed individuals and peoples'.[10]

So if we are to consider mass movements of class struggle as moved by the Spirit, what might we learn about those who catalyse and lead these movements? How might we view those voices crying out in the wilderness to prepare the way of the Lord? In the next section I will explore these questions through considering the role of the Spirit in the ministry of prophets – those who lead through foretelling and *forth*telling what is, or might be, to come.

The Spirit and the voice of the prophets

When John's messengers had gone, Jesus began to speak to the crowds about John: 'What did you go out into the wilderness to look at? A reed shaken by the wind? What then did you go out to see? Someone dressed in soft robes? Look, those who put on fine clothing and live in luxury are in royal palaces. What then did you go out to see? A prophet? Yes, I tell you, and more than a prophet.' (Luke 7.24–26 NRSV)

For a significant chunk of my early Christian formation, a prophet was often someone who would stand up in a church service, point at someone, and say something like, 'I see a picture of a calm stream which is God's peace flowing into your heart.' Why the metaphors were always something to do with water I never quite figured out. During one of the most memorable lectures I had during my undergraduate studies in theology, the speaker read some choice passages from the prophets of the Old Testament, each followed by a similarly trite 'blessed thought' to the one I have just described. The point was not lost on any of us – the prophecy of biblical tradition is profoundly radical and profoundly practical, raging against injustice and the unfaithfulness of God's people. We might consider the following passages as particularly relevant examples in our own time:

'Woe to those who make iniquitous decrees,
who write oppressive statutes,
to turn aside the needy from justice
and to rob the poor of my people of their right,
to make widows their spoil
and to plunder orphans!'
(Isaiah 10.1–2 NRSV)

Then I will draw near to you for judgement; I will be swift
to bear witness against the sorcerers, against the adulterers,
against those who swear falsely, against those who oppress
the hired workers in their wages, the widow, and the orphan,
against those who thrust aside the alien, and do not fear me,
says the LORD of hosts. (Malachi 3.5 NRSV)

The prophets speak by the fire of the Spirit about the journey from the world as it is to the world as it should be. Not
through trite platitudes, but in addressing specific material,
economic and labour relationships. Not a watery metaphor in
sight (although I'll concede Amos 5.24 – 'let justice roll down
like waters'). Some have described this prophetic ministry as
'speaking truth to power', a phrase also used by non-religious
activists. Speaking truth to power is, of course, a dangerous
business. It didn't work out well for people like John the Baptist, who ended up with his head on a platter for his troubles.
Prophets, by their very nature, are disruptive of the status
quo. They are like salt in the wounds of society, cleaning but
irritating in the process. Jesus recognized this in the passage I
quoted above, when he contrasted John the Baptist with those
who wear soft robes and live in palaces. Prophets, it seems, are
rarely those who speak from positions of societal or institutional power and privilege.

In Chapter 5, Selina Stone describes how we might see the
early Pentecostal movement as a prophetic challenge to the
established Church of England in recognizing the Spirit's calling and equipping of all people, regardless of class, race or
gender. This prophetic challenge goes beyond the mere reform-
ing of church leadership structures, but rather is a prophetic

challenge to disrupt the forces of racism, class oppression and colonialism that cause untold misery to God's children. In her chapter, Mother Kath Long recognizes how badly the Church of England continues to fail and silence those called to ministry from working-class backgrounds, pointing out that many of us do not fit the stereotypical image of the nice white-middle-class vicar caricatured in popular television shows such as *The Vicar of Dibley*. The experiences Mother Kath shares from her own research resonate with my own experiences of discernment, training and deployment in the Church of England. I enjoyed much of my training, and I am extremely grateful for being given access to an education I could never have dreamed of, but I couldn't (and still can't) escape the feeling that my face just didn't fit. Here, class issues of course intersect with race and many other locations of oppression. I remember, during an excellent conference on 'Decolonising Theological Education' held at Cuddesdon, Professor Anthony Reddie turning to me and saying, 'They didn't have people like me and you in mind when they built this place!' There are, of course, notable exceptions to this, where colleges and courses were specifically developed to train people for ministry from working-class backgrounds, but this was sometimes done with a highly paternalistic mindset that among other things included elocution lessons and assumed lack of intellectual ability. The story of the working-class priest Father Joe Williamson, which predates my own experiences by almost a century, could have been written yesterday. Father Joe, who grew up in the slums of Poplar and Stepney, had a troublous time in the Church of England, despite his remarkable ministry. He wrote:

> The system was and still is cock-eyed, and it has nothing to do with real vocation. God wanted me, and for a priest. He was not to be frustrated by tinpot people who were running the Church by class distinction, intellectual class distinction.[11]

It is my belief that in excluding and frustrating the voices of a variety of working-class people, the Church of England (and other established/'mainline' denominations) plugs its ears to prophetic challenges that would bring transformation. Those who are anointed by the Spirit to bring prophetic fire are rarely those in soft robes and fine palaces, but rather those who wander the wilderness. The danger for those of us who find our way to the outside edge of the inside circle is that the process of formation can often seek to knock off those rough edges that God has given us as gifts to the Church. Willie James Jennings observes this in critiquing the desired end product of Christian 'formation' for ministry: 'a white self-sufficient man, his self-sufficiency defined by possession, control and mastery'.[12] Possession, control and mastery are, in my opinion, middle-class values and attributes that do not sit well with those from working-class backgrounds. I'm encouraged to see working-class leaders like Bishop Lynne Cullens move into positions of authority and influence in the Church of England while maintaining an outspoken critique of existing class relationships. But the challenge to those of us in any key-holding position is to keep discerning where the Spirit is working, and who the Spirit is raising up to bring new leadership and change. The danger is that those of us who find ourselves in growing proximity to power and privilege (particularly through our positions in church and academic institutions) drown out the voices of those less proximate, those experiencing multiple barriers to having a voice. Those of us gaining a voice and a seat at the table must allow the Spirit to ask us (in the words of Gayatri Spivak): 'Can the subaltern speak?'[13] Recognizing the close relationship between class intersectionality and knowledge production calls us again to solidarity. Solidarity in particular with those enduring the most hideous and exploitative economic and labour relations that maintain the lifestyles of many of us in the West.

It is interesting that Jennings grounds the prophetic call of his book in reaching for a theological education (or ministry training) that is a 'formation in communion'.[14] This too is the work of the Spirit, forming leaders orientated to and leading towards the solidarity of communion. As inhabitants of the 'Capitalocene', this formation in 'global solidarities', as Catherine Keller puts it, might be the only hope for our species.[15] Keller's call should point us outward in expectation to discern the voice of the

Spirit among those voices outside the Church that are calling for global solidarities. I for one would be amenable to inviting Mick Lynch or many of the other voices quoted in this book to the pulpit in my parish. This view of prophecy transcends the idea of 'speaking truth to power' – the danger being, as the saying goes, that 'We keep the truth and they keep the power.' Prophets are rarely those with power and prestige; they often occupy the liminal spaces and the wilderness. Prophetic leaders who call us towards the solidarity of communion – both inside and outside the Christian tradition – are prophets who both foretell and *forth*tell – they take us from the world as it is to the world as it should be.

Organizing as a *missio Spiritus*

In the first chapter I quoted a motto from the field of working-class studies – 'We gather not to mourn, but to organise.'[16] Organizing is, for me, a relational approach to the journey from the world as it is to the world as it should be. This happens through people coming together to build diverse people-power, joining together in the kind of mass movements of solidarity I have described, raising up leaders who can take us through the wilderness and taking action to move power holders and decision makers towards the common good. A key understanding from pneumatology is that the work of the Spirit is to transform relationships and foster deeper relationality. In his classic book, the former missionary and Anglican Bishop John V. Taylor refers to the Spirit as the 'Go-Between God', recognizing the Spirit's ministry as having both interpersonal and socio-economic implications 'in the service we can render together to the world'.[17] As I have already suggested, it is my firm belief that the Spirit of God is at work among those movements of solidarity that lead the human race towards a brighter future. Organizing for change ultimately means a transformation of the way people relate to each other, non-human life and the rest of creation. If, then, part of the Spirit's work is to transform the way people relate to one another and to God, binding us together in communion (as we see in the first chapters of Acts), what are the implications for our understanding of mission?

Many global theologians are turning to theologies of the Holy Spirit as a place to explore missiology, ecclesiology, dialogue between faiths and economic and ecological justice. These categories, of course, all overlap. There are examples of this in all sorts of strands of theology, whether it is Roman Catholic theology of religions post-Vatican II; the theologies that have accompanied civil rights movements in the USA and elsewhere over the last 70 years; even, God forbid, in some of the mission documents that have come out of the Church of England in recent years. Some of the most ground-breaking work exploring the intersection of mission, pneumatology and justice has been done by the Malaysian-American theologian Amos Yong. Yong argues that from the post-Pentecost perspective of Acts 2, the *missio Spiritus* (mission of the Spirit) emphasizes the socio-economic domain.[18] This transformation of socio-economic relationships, in Yong's view, is not limited to the internal relationships of the early Christians who 'had all things in common' and redistributed their wealth (Acts 2.44–45). But rather these transformed relationships reflect the wider biblical tradition of caring for the alien and the stranger and seeking 'the welfare of the city' (Jeremiah 29.7). Yong sees the Spirit's mission as 'the interrelational work of the divine life that creates, sustains, and redeems the world and in that respect interfaces with others at and beyond the so-called borders of the believing community'.[19] As Yong recognizes, the socio-economic and the political are intertwined, therefore there is a strong political element to the *missio Spiritus* both in terms of the local and the international. It is here that the work of Yong and many others on reimagining interfaith solidarity through the Spirit becomes so essential. Again, the witness to 'planetary justice' that the Spirit inspired in the prophets comes into view, a 'prophetic kerygma of justice and righteousness so needed for a late modern world replete with injustice'.[20] This turn to the Spirit helps us reimagine our relationships of solidarity and organize for change with allies of all faiths and none. It is essential both on the global stage and in the religiously diverse urban communities of Britain, the places where I and other contributors to this book conduct our ministry, activism and research. Indeed, an aspect of feckless faith I did not cover in the first chapter is a faith that cannot adequately engage with the challenges of religiously plural postcolonial contexts. The Sri Lankan liberation theologian Aloysius Pieris recognizes with great clarity that the vast majority of 'God's poor' belong to religions other than Christianity. This is true in Pieris' Sri Lankan context, but also in many of our British contexts too. With this in mind, Pieris argues, 'a theology that does not speak to or speak through this non-Christian peoplehood is an esoteric luxury of a Christian minority.'[21] A turn to the Spirit and the praxis of liberation have been, in my experience at least, a chance to discover mutually fulfilling and transformative relationships with people of other faiths.

These more recent turns to the Spirit in missiology and other disciplines have a far older and more enigmatic counterpart in the relationship between revolutionary politics and the visions of the twelfth-century abbot Joachim of Fiore. Catherine Keller points to this history of Joachim's vision of an 'Age of the Spirit' when 'church hierarchy would fall away, as all would have direct access to God. All goods would be held communally, as in the agapic communism of the first generation of Christians.'[22] Fiore's legacy is nuanced; his original writings show little in the way of revolutionary drive. But ideas have a habit of forming lives of their own. As Matthias Riedl demonstrates in his excellent essay on Fiore, the development of the revolutionary idea of a 'third age', an 'uprising of the underprivileged against the ruling classes, ecclesiastical as well as secular', can be traced from Fiore, via radical Franciscanism, to the key thinkers of modern communism, including Friedrich Engels.[23] Here I must sound a note of caution, however, because both extreme left- and extreme right-wing movements of the twentieth century took at least some inspiration from the imaginary and terminology of Fiore, including the Nazis in their conception of a 'third Reich' (albeit rather loosely and with less historical development than in the case of Communism).[24] Where love and solidarity cease to be at the centre, these utopian 'third age' dreams of the Spirit can quite easily descend into totalitarian nightmares, whether right or left. Discernment, then, becomes a key priority.

With this in mind as we come to a close, what might all of this look like in practice? Sally Mann, Victoria Turner and Eve Parker have demonstrated in their chapters that this call of the Spirit to class justice and solidarity is present in the world of work and labour relationships, in church mission to the working classes, and in the arena of theological education. Each has masterfully pointed towards the need for change, be it through practical approaches to challenging economies of precarity and 'bullshit jobs', challenging churches to rediscover radical approaches to mission among working-class communities, and challenging theological education establishments to educate for class consciousness. If we are to believe, then, that 'where the Spirit of the Lord is, there is freedom' means something more than personal piety, how might Christians join in the *missio Spiritus* today? I agree wholeheartedly with Rieger that: 'The organic work of movement and community organising [becomes] one of the most genuine expressions of the faith of religious communities and therefore key to the work of theology in the Capitalocene.'[25]

I offer, in closing, three brief suggestions for practical ways in which many Christians, churches and Christian organizations could consider responding to the Spirit and moving from mourning to organizing.

Broad-based organizing and the real Living Wage

I have tried to argue that to move beyond feckless faith our theology of class must have proper practical implications that impact upon labour relationships. In Britain's cost-of-living crisis of 2022, the problem of low wages has once again been brought to the public eye. Class justice starts, at least, with fair wages being paid for fair work. That many of the 'key' workers we clapped and cheered for in the pandemic are now reliant on foodbanks is a source of national shame. Many people are fighting back in solidarity with broad-based alliances organizing to support the Real Living Wage Campaign. Since 2016, the campaign has calculated the realistic levels of pay needed to meet the cost of basic living standards from one year to the next, recognizing that a government-set minimum wage and a real Living Wage are not the same thing. With the support of allies in broad-based community organizing alliances, including faith communities, trade unions and other civil society institutions like schools, they have won over £1.3 billion pounds into the pockets of the lowest-paid workers in Britain. In my own local ministry and organizing work, low wages has repeatedly come up as an issue, which has led me to take part in this campaign myself. There are also wider possibilities for what can be won through broad-based organizing, lobbying government and other power holders, both locally and nationally, particularly in relation to issues that affect the working classes such as housing, education and investment in community infrastructure. I believe that we are only in the early stages of seeing what might be possible in the UK and should dream big about the justice wins that people can achieve when they come together.

Winning a real Living Wage for an increasing number of workers is a tangible way in which churches and Christian organizations can take part in the *missio Spiritus* by entering into greater socio-economic solidarity with our own members and our neighbours of all faiths and none. Worthwhile as this is, however, the impact has its limits. Winning a real Living Wage does little to fundamentally alter the labour relationships and lack of access to the means of production that lead to the exploitation of workers. It can, however, make a huge difference in the short term to the lives of millions of people.

Trade union organizing

As I have already described in this chapter, unions are once again in the public eye. That nurses and ambulance drivers are at the time of writing striking en masse for the first time ever in the UK, alongside continued murmurings of a general strike, is something theologians and Christian leaders ought to pay attention to. I am disappointed to see such little outspoken support for the unions from Christian leaders, especially considering the historic relationships between labour movements and Christianity in England and the role of key figures such as the former Bishop of Durham, David Jenkins, who supported miners during the major strikes of 1984–5. While an increasing number of Church of England clergy are joining the Faith Workers Branch of Unite the Union, I still think we have a long way to go in terms of supporting real union organizing for better labour relationships. This comes into clearer view when we consider our relationships with academic institutions through the role of theological education in the formation of church leaders. Academics have been at the forefront of this year's strike action in the context of the neo-liberalization of education and the casualization of academic work. Shocking as it may sound, many junior academics are now in a very real sense among the throng of precariat workers who live hand-to-mouth, just like I did on the building site (albeit in a slightly warmer and safer environment). It is again important to remember that to be working class is mainly about labour conditions and relationships, not necessarily doing manual work or the way people dress or speak.[26] This gradual proletarianization of traditionally 'middle strata' jobs (which is a symptom of capitalism) makes it in the interests of a significant proportion of the middle classes to enter into solidarity with the class and labour struggles.[27] As Rieger suggests, as the power of capital grows and is consolidated into a shrinking group of elites known as the '1%', the '99%' working and middle classes have a growing need to find solidarity and organize with each other.[28] The acceleration of innovation through technologies such as artificial intelligence/machine learning and robotics is likely to hasten this trend in what some are calling a 'Fourth Industrial Revolution'. Keller points to the negative impact that this will probably have on the labouring masses in her apocalyptic dream-reading of the near-future.[29] This needs developing through further theological reflection, which is beyond the scope of this book; however, I believe an intersectional class analysis should be a high priority, given that 'the

Fourth Industrial Revolution can shift even more power from labour towards capital and increase the levels of precariousness beyond those already experienced'.[30] While not always overtly critical of capitalist economics, many contemporary commentators and futurists seem to agree on the risks that technological innovations pose to proletariat workers.[31]

Faith leaders can play a significant role in union movements, and this came starkly into view for me when the workers in a local charity I visited for chaplaincy disclosed the strain they feel while being paid the minimum wage for demanding, traumatic and essential work supporting some of the most vulnerable in our community. Lack of charity funds didn't seem to be the issue, just the way they were being distributed. This is where the role of religious leaders in offering pastoral care in the Capitalocene becomes challenging. While of course I offered support and a listening ear, I also encouraged the workers to consider unionizing for better pay, conditions and support, and contacted the relevant branch representative at my union. Whether this will be fruitful only time will tell. Some may feel uncomfortable that I have acted in this way, but I'm reminded again of the words of the RMT Union chairperson Mick Lynch, who responded to the current Bishop of Durham's criticism of their strike action by saying, 'What does he want us to do, pray?' I do, of course, pray for my friends at this charity, but sometimes prayer alone is not enough.

I think that those of us who are able should join the trade union movement as dues-paying members to help build strength and solidarity, but I don't think we should stop there. I think we really need to get organized and start dreaming bigger about how we can begin to push back properly and shift labour relationships in the direction of justice. There are weaknesses in the trade union culture of the UK; sometimes unions get stuck in their representative role of service delivery and lose their radical politics. There is also much to be critiqued about the relationship between unions and the current iteration of the 'Labour' party, whose champagne socialism seems to offer little substantive challenge to the exploitation of workers and other oppressed groups under capitalism.[32] I know some people would consider this sort of action and discourse too 'political' and too 'adversarial' for nice Christians to get tied up in. In response I would turn to the epistle of James:

> Come now, you rich people, weep and wail for the miseries that are coming to you. Your riches have rotted, and your clothes are moth-eaten. Your gold and silver have rusted, and their rust will be evidence against you, and it will eat your flesh like fire. You have laid up treasure during the last days. Listen! The wages of the labourers who mowed your fields, which you kept back by fraud, cry out, and the cries of the harvesters have reached the ears of the Lord of hosts. (James 5.1–4 NRSV)

Organizing alternatives through cooperatives

The third option I want to suggest is one that I am only just beginning to explore myself, but one which I think offers genuine transformative potential: the use of cooperatives and other democratized structures to create fairer alternative workplaces and other institutions. While the UK has a long history of credit unions (democratically run and member-owned financial institutions) and worker cooperatives (democratically run and worker-owned businesses), there is still potential here waiting to be unlocked. When we consider the potential resources and influence that churches and other faith communities can bring, it's exciting to imagine what could be achieved. Cooperatives offer workers or credit union members the chance to have much more 'skin in the game' by giving them control of how surplus profit is used and how the business functions. The interests of workers as a body become the driving force of the organization rather than the interests of bosses, shareholders or capital investors. Like broad-based organizing and union organizing, I believe this also creates an environment where solidarity can thrive and the most vulnerable will be better protected as a result. I am once again indebted to the work of Rosemarie and Joerg Rieger and the Wendland-Cook Program in Religion and

Justice for their ground-breaking work on this topic, and would recommend both their courses and their book *United We Are A Force* for further reflection.[33] There is no need to repeat these ideas at length here, other than to say that it would be exciting to see faith communities in the UK begin to organize for justice in this way, creating good jobs with good pay in the process. Imagine if every cathedral cafe was a worker co-op, with a prayer card for every table that said, 'We have bread, others have none, God bless the revolution.' A guy can dream, right?!

A closing prayer for imagination

My hope is that churches, Christian organizations and Christian people will allow the Spirit of God and the voices of the prophets to expand our imagination for what is possible, leading us into movements of greater solidarity with allies of all faiths and none in the class struggle. The more established Western churches, I believe, can only play their part if their imagination expands. As Walter Brueggemann rightly says: 'It is the vocation of the prophet to keep alive the ministry of imagination, to keep on conjuring and proposing futures.'[34] While many churches and faith communities in the UK work tirelessly for charitable aims, we do well to heed the words of the American pastor and organizer Dennis Jacobsen: 'Society is pleased to have the church exhaust itself in being merciful toward the casualties of unjust systems.'[35] Charity is, quite simply, not enough. Otherwise, as Archbishop Stephen Cottrell so masterfully put it, it will always be 'hand-outs', and never 'hand-ups' that actually lift people out of the poverty brought on by unjust economic and political systems.[36]

It's commonly said that people find it easier to believe in the end of the world than in the end of capitalism. In the long view, then, it seems to me that nothing short of a total upheaval of our present political, economic and labour relations will bring about the kinds of changes needed to win justice for the oppressed classes of our nation and our world. The radical

Colombian priest and organizer Camilo Torres challenged Christians in his homeland:

> If beneficence, alms, the few tuition-free schools, the few housing projects – in general what is known as 'charity' do not succeed in feeding the hungry majority, clothing the naked, or teaching the unschooled masses, we must seek effective means to achieve the well-being of these majorities.[37]

The practices I have suggested above can be just that, a *means* to achieve change. It is important, then, that we recognize the limits of these and other tools to shift the whole system towards justice. What they certainly can do is win short-term justice gains for the working classes, which is of course worthwhile. But more than this, they can create spaces to build intersectional solidarity between the labouring classes and incubate the tools and experiences needed for democratic participation in production and power that these classes require to win justice.[38] They can also cultivate that most dangerous tool of the working classes: hope.

Ultimately, I am coming to believe that a revolution of solidarity and a shifting of the balance of power is our only hope for real change. The word 'revolution' is one that makes many Christians nervous, not least because of the religious oppression and violence associated with some historic revolutions, including, of course, 'left wing' ones. But empowered by the Spirit we might imagine a different kind of revolution that is no less concrete in its effect. We might, like Mary mother of Jesus, imagine by the Spirit a revolution where the mighty are cast down from their thrones and the lowly lifted up, the hungry fed and the rich sent empty away (Luke 1.52–53). That we repeat this prayer daily in many Christian traditions and yet are so scared of the idea of revolution should tell us how captive our imaginations have become.

I close this book, therefore, with a few lines from the *Veni Creator Spiritus*, which is sung in many Roman Catholic and Anglican churches as an invocation of the Spirit on occasions such as baptisms and ordinations. I invite all Christians, in view of our baptismal oaths and/or the duties of ministerial office, to pray these words that the Spirit might open our minds to imagine new horizons of the possible:

Come, Holy Ghost, our souls inspire,
and lighten with celestial fire.
Thou the anointing Spirit art,
who dost thy sevenfold gifts impart.

Thy blessed unction from above
is comfort, life, and fire of love.
Enable with perpetual light
the dullness of our blinded sight.

Anoint and cheer our soiled face
with the abundance of thy grace.
Keep far our foes, give peace at home:
where thou art guide, no ill can come.

Teach us to know the Father, Son,
and thee, of both, to be but One,
that through the ages all along,
this may be our endless song:

Praise to thy eternal merit,
Father, Son, and Holy Spirit.

Notes

1 Harry Bridges (Founding Leader of the International Longshore and Warehouse Union).

2 Anthony Reddie, 2019, *Theologising Brexit: A Liberationist and Postcolonial Critique*, Routledge New Critical Thinking in Religion, Theology and Biblical Studies, London and New York: Routledge, p. 169.

3 See the Migrants Organise website: www.migrantsorganise.org.

4 Rowan Williams, 'Solidarity: The 2021 Ken Leech Memorial Lecture', 15.11.2021 (manuscript), p. 5.

5 Williams, 'Solidarity', p. 6.

6 Rowan Williams, 2022, 'No One is Safe until Everyone is Safe – We Applied it to the Pandemic, but Why Not Our Economy?', *The Guardian*, 31 December, https://www.theguardian.com/commentisfree/2022/dec/31/safe-pandemic-economy-cost-of-living-crisis (accessed 9.01.2023).

7 Timothy Gorringe, 1994, *Alan Ecclestone: Priest as Revolutionary*, Sheffield: Cairns Publications, pp. 22–3.

8 Gorringe, *Alan Ecclestone*, p. 26.

9 Sergius Bulgakov, 2004, *The Comforter*, Grand Rapids, MI: William B. Eerdmans, p. 284.

10 Jorge V. Pixley, 1987, *On Exodus: A Liberation Perspective*, Maryknoll, NY: Orbis Books, p. xiv.

11 Joe Williamson, 1963, *Father Joe*, St Helens: Wood Westworth & Co., p. 101.

12 Willie James Jennings, 2020, *After Whiteness: An Education in Belonging*, Grand Rapids, MI: William B. Eerdmans, p. 6.

13 Gayatri Chakravorty Spivak, 'Can The Subaltern Speak', *Die Philosophin*, 14.27 (1988), p. 94.

14 Jennings, *After Whiteness*, p. 108.

15 Catherine Keller, 2021, 'Spiritual Foundations of One World', *Contribution to GTI Forum Can Human Solidarity Globalize?*, https://greattransition.org/gti-forum/global-solidarity-keller (accessed 22.03.2023).

16 Michele Fazio et al., 2021, *Routledge International Handbook of Working-Class Studies*, Abingdon and New York: Routledge, p. 1.

17 John V. Taylor, 2021, *The Go-Between God*, new edition, London: SCM Press, p. 241.

18 Amos Yong, 2019, *Mission after Pentecost*, Grand Rapids, MI: Baker Academic, p. 278.

19 Yong, *Mission after Pentecost*, p. 278.

20 Yong, *Mission after Pentecost*, p. 279.

21 Aloysius Pieris, 1988, *An Asian Theology of Liberation*, Edinburgh: T & T Clark, p. 87.

22 Catherine Keller, 2021, *Facing Apocalypse: Climate, Democracy, and Other Last Chances* Maryknoll, NY: Orbis Books, p. 169.

23 Matthias Riedl, 2018, 'Longing for the Third Age: Revolutionary Joachism, Communism, and National Socialism', in *A Companion to Joachim of Fiore*, ed. Matthias Riedl, Leiden: Brill, pp. 275, 298–300.

24 Riedl, 'Longing for the Third Age', p. 304.

25 Joerg Rieger, 2022, *Theology in the Capitalocene: Ecology, Identity, Class, and Solidarity*, Minneapolis, MN: Fortress Press, pp. 12–13.

26 An important recognition made by the Italian Marxist philosopher Antonio Gramsci: Antonio Gramsci, 2012, *Selections from the Prison Notebooks of Antonio Gramsci*, London: Lawrence & Wishart, p. 8.

27 See Rosa Luxemburg, 2020, *Reform or Revolution?*, Paris: Foreign Languages Press, p. 54.

28 Rieger, *Capitalocene*, pp. 72–3.

29 Keller, *Facing Apocalypse*, pp. 221–2.

30 Carl Hughes and Alan Southern, 'The World of Work and the Crisis of Capitalism: Marx and the Fourth Industrial Revolution', *Journal of Classical Sociology*, 19.1 (2019), p. 62.

31 For example, see Erik Brynjolfsson and Andrew McAfee, 2014, *The Second Machine Age: Work, Progress, and Prosperity in a Time of Brilliant Technologies*, New York: W. W. Norton & Company, pp. 107–24; and Yuval Noah Harari, 2016, *Homo Deus: A Brief History of Tomorrow*, London: Harvill Secker, pp. 30–5.

32 For an in-depth analysis of this, see Solidarity Federation, 2012, *Fighting for Ourselves: Anarcho-Syndicalism and the Class Struggle*, Great Britain: Solidarity Federation and Freedom Press, pp. 11–28.

33 Joerg Rieger and Rosemarie Henkel-Rieger, 2016, *Unified we are a Force: How Faith and Labor Can Overcome America's Inequalities*, St Louis, MO: Chalice Press.

34 Walter Brueggemann, 2018, *The Prophetic Imagination*, Minneapolis, MN: Fortress Press, p. 40.

35 Dennis A. Jacobsen, 2017, *Doing Justice: Congregations and Community Organizing*, Minneapolis, MN: Fortress Press, p. 28.

36 From his sermon at the Sunday service of the Labour Party Conference, 2022.

37 Camilo Torres and John Gerassi, 1971, *Revolutionary Priest: The Complete Writings and Messages of Camilo Torres*, New York: Vintage Books, p. 374.

38 There is not space to elaborate further here, but chapters 7 and 8 of Rosa Luxemburg's *Reform or Revolution* clearly and concisely demonstrate how organizing, unions and co-ops can contribute to longer-term class justice.

Afterword

JOERG RIEGER, DISTINGUISHED
PROFESSOR OF THEOLOGY,
VANDERBILT UNIVERSITY

Those who work their way through this book will be rewarded with a plethora of reflections and insights that continue to be surprisingly absent in most theological and ecclesial conversations. This is certainly true on both sides of the North Atlantic Ocean, even though theologians and church leaders have become somewhat more open to some of the concerns of our times in recent years.

Why matters of social class and solidarity are under-reflected in current discourses has various reasons, many of which I have investigated elsewhere.[1] Suffice it to say here that serious study of the flows of power are always complex and difficult endeavours, especially when they point to what shapes us unconsciously to our very cores and when they come up with real-life solutions that have actual track records of 'confounding the mighty'.[2]

What I want to address here, though, are the substantial gains that grow out of reflections on social class and solidarity, not only for the world as a whole but also for religious communities. This book illustrates some of these gains well, but there are other gains that are just now re-emerging after a period of long silence. Allow me to name four of these gains that are addressed in this book.

First is a new level of self-awareness. The authors demonstrate the importance of understanding themselves in the context of the flow of power that includes class as well as other (often imposed) markers of identity, such as race, caste and gender. Note that becoming aware of one's class location is not merely a matter of autobiography but tied to communities and emerging solidarity. As a result, this project is not primarily individuals developing levels of class consciousness that are virtually absent in faith communities – it is a matter of understanding oneself in light of the communities that shaped us and activating these understandings for the common good. The result is a broadened understanding of self and a broadened understanding of faith and world, with a new awareness of the contributions of those who are ignored (whose labour built Rome, our cities, the cathedrals?). In sum, the working class – which is not a minority but remains the majority of society both in the UK and in the USA – has deep insights into existential matters of life and death that affect us all, including the middle class and even the executive class.

Second are deepened understandings of class that connect the chapters of this book with some of the work that we have been doing in the United States through the Wendland-Cook Program in Religion and Justice at Vanderbilt University, and the Class, Theology and Religion unit at the American Academy of Religion, and in many related publications. Class, we are beginning to rediscover, is ultimately a matter of relationship between classes. This relationship is marked by tensions and struggles, which tend to benefit the few rather than the many. The common sense that the poor are getting poorer and the rich are getting richer does not refer to some lamentable accident but is part of how our current socio-economic system works, where 'winner takes all', or at least as much as possible. It is for this reason that prevalent theories of class that examine matters of social stratification and social status are of limited benefit for this discussion, as they tend to downplay or ignore the relational aspect of class. Even some notions of 'classism' diminish this relational aspect if class is merely defined in terms of stereotypes and prejudice rather than of exploitation. Of course, it is precisely this relational aspect that makes class such an important part of the study of theology and the life of faith. Here too everything is relational, including human encounters of the divine, which is another reason why skewed class relationships are so profoundly damaging. When class struggle is a way of life (not because Karl Marx made note of it but because so many of the 99% who have to work for a living experience its pressures every single day), relationships to other people, to the planet and even to God are inevitably distorted as well – often to such a degree that religion is turned into its very opposite.

Third is a new engagement of the intersectionalities of various forms of exploitation and oppression. In contrast to common suspicions, engaging class does not have to mean paying less attention to the tensions of race, ethnicity, gender and sexuality. Just the opposite, as I have argued in my own work: attending to the tensions of class, which are part of all of our lives under the conditions of global capitalism, can deepen awareness of the systemic nature of racism and sexism and their use in stabilizing unjust flows of power. Based on our experiences in the United States, it can be argued that racism and sexism are intentionally used to cover up people's awareness of class, misleading white working people who are unaware of their class to believe they have more in common with members of the white executive class than with non-white working people. Renewed awareness of class and class solidarity, therefore, can help people address and fight racism and sexism in profound and lasting ways. Theologians and faith communities have much to learn here, which is another reason why the work presented in this book could be so important.

Fourth, and perhaps most exciting for those who are interested in positive contributions of faith in today's world, are fresh insights into the mission and ministry of the church, with implications for interreligious relations as well. The individual chapters provide significant insights in this regard, developed in the contexts of actual ministry, from which I will continue to learn and which in some cases match the work that we are doing in the United States.[3] This is where the notion of solidarity acquires new importance. To be sure, the solidarity at work here is not the right-wing solidarity that promotes homogeneity and marching in lockstep, but the solidarity of those who experience the pressures of the current age in their own bodies (this has substantial implications for interreligious dialogue as well, which cannot be further elaborated here). These considerations bring us back to the agency and even the leadership of those who are affected the most by these pressures, which are the members of the working-class majority, which today is the most diverse body of people in the world, whose plight is exacerbated by racism and sexism. But – and more work needs to be done here – this now also includes the middle class. To clarify: while the middle class appears to be firmly in charge in the church, it is ultimately not the class in control either. In fact, middle-class people also have to work for a living and have bosses, not unlike the working class, but their relation to the working class is obscured by a mostly mistaken sense that the interests of the middle and the executive classes coincide. In other words, the middle class too has more of an interest in 'confounding the mighty' than is often realized – even in faith communities – and can therefore become an organic part of the solidarity that is at the heart of this volume.

In conclusion, I am grateful to this group of theologians for tackling the complex and difficult topics of faith communities, social class and solidarity. There are differences between our contexts – perhaps some forms of working-class identity are still more alive in the UK than in the USA, perhaps the aristocracy has more of a hold on the church in the UK – but the parallels are hard to overlook: what drives not only the fate of the planet (including the environment) but also faith communities are the interests of a surprisingly small minority that has managed to make many of us believe that their interests are our interests. This is at the heart of the so-called American Dream (from rags to riches), which covers up the fact that upward social mobility is a pipe dream, as the US population is now less socially mobile than even the population of Britain.[4]

The solution, of course, is not to lament or to lay blame on (mighty) individuals but to develop new kinds of relationships with each other and the divine. But – as the stories of this book convey to us in various ways – such relationships cannot be developed without fundamentally addressing labour relationships, political relationships and the relationships of race, ethnicity, gender and sexuality. In the end, solidarity amounts to relationships that are truly cooperative at all levels, and perhaps it is indeed worker cooperatives that at present most fully embody what has the power to transform communities – including communities of faith as well as interfaith – from the bottom up.[5]

Notes

1 Joerg Rieger, 2022, *Theology in the Capitalocene: Ecology, Identity, Class, and Solidarity*, Minneapolis, MN: Fortress Press; chapter 3 deals with religion and class; chapter 4 deals with religion and intersectionality.

2 The labour movement offers an example of such real-life solutions, as its successes are actually quite tangible and are surprisingly closely related to faith communities over the past several centuries. Those who appreciate 40-hour work weeks, the end of child labour, women's rights at work and worker protections and benefits, owe a debt of gratitude to coalitions of labour and religion, especially in the United States.

3 See, for instance, the work of the Solidarity Circles initiated by the Wendland-Cook Program in Religion and Justice at Vanderbilt University (https://www.religionandjustice.org/solidarity-circles).

4 Alissa Quart, 2018, 'What Americans Can Learn from British Class Guilt', *The Guardian*, 28 March, https://www.theguardian.com/us-news/2018/mar/28/which-country-has-the-worst-class-system-the-uk-or-us (accessed 22.03.2023).

5 See the work of the Southeast Center of Cooperative Development in Nashville on faith and coops (https://www.co-opsnow.org/tool-kit).